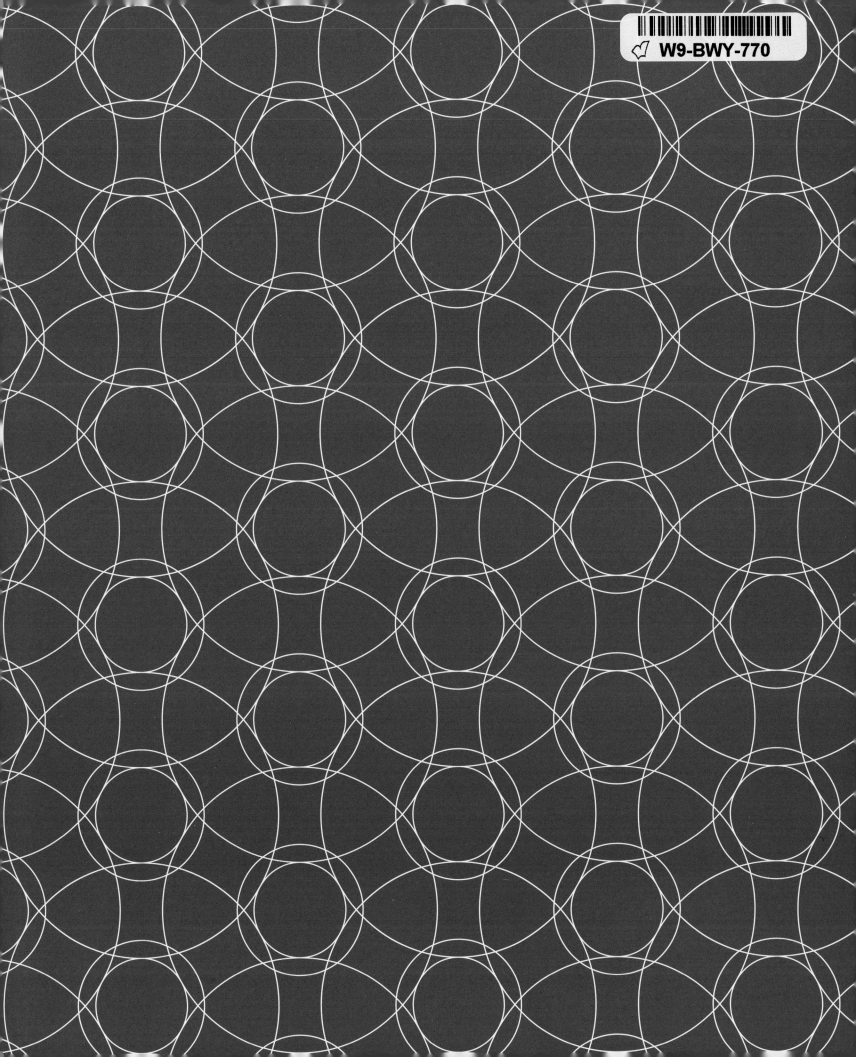

Nicholas Bowen

REGENT'S
UNIVERSITY LONDON
100 YEARS OF HIGHER EDUCATION IN REGENT'S PARK

MERRELL
LONDON · NEW YORK

Contents

Foreword

Ian Mehrtens, Pro-Chancellor of the University and Chair of the Board of Trustees, addresses the audience at the University's inaugural event on 29 June 2013.

For a century, from the establishment of Bedford College in the park, through the foundation of Regent's College and on to Regent's University London today, the Inner Circle campus has been a centre for innovative and important higher education. The Trustee Board, staff, students and alumni of the University are proud to be part of the Regent's family, and are committed to its future growth and recognition as the leading internationally focused, private, non-state-funded, not-for-profit university in Europe and beyond.

Our enviable setting in Regent's Park provides a peaceful and secure environment for study. The park is also conveniently close to all the business, cultural and social locations that are offered by one of the world's greatest cosmopolitan cities. We are at the heart of the Regent's Park educational village, and our neighbours include the Royal Academy of Music, the London Business School, the Royal College of Physicians, the Royal College of Obstetricians and Gynaecologists, the Zoological Society of London, the Open Air Theatre and the Prince's Trust.

Successive teams have built on the foundations laid by Bedford for a first-class educational experience, centred on individual needs and resulting in readiness for a successful career in the students' chosen fields. The international approach and the focus on languages and culture alongside specialist subjects, developed during the early years of Regent's College, are still very much characteristics that set us aside from other universities in the United Kingdom. Our diverse student population, drawn from more than 140 nationalities, ensures that learners work together and develop a global perspective.

We are completely private and receive no money from government. We believe strongly in public benefit and, despite continual pressure from potential investors, maintain our commitment to remaining a charity, using all our funds to further refresh and develop our students' learning experience and long-term success.

A century of higher education on this site is a moment to mark. If you have never visited us, please come and see what we mean when we say to our students, 'Regent's University: your world of difference'.

Ian Mehrtens

PRO-CHANCELLOR AND CHAIR OF REGENT'S UNIVERSITY LONDON BOARD OF TRUSTEES

Introduction

Regent's University London is a unique institution, focused on being 'Independent, International and Socially Responsible'. We provide a very different experience for our students – one that prepares them for working in an increasingly global market in every sector from business to theatre, fashion to energy management. Our international students build networks and relationships that stand the test of time and provide help and support for life.

In this book, we pay tribute to those who pioneered a special approach to higher education that focuses on the individual, and which has led us to be the institution we are today, from the opening by Her Majesty Queen Mary in July 1913 in Regent's Park of Bedford College under the leadership of Margaret Tuke, through the award of full university title to Regent's University London in 2013.

Our progress is a complex story to relate, and progress has required contribution from many. Regent's thinks of itself as a family that includes its Trustees, staff and students, past and present, and our international partners. You will see from these pages that it is considered a pleasant and valuable place to study. When interviewed for the book, one of the legends of the campus, William Carbury, who has worked here since 1985, recalled some of the highlights of his career and explained the main reason why he has stayed so long: 'Regent's College is like a shoe you put on that is so comfortable.'

The experience here is comfortable, but it is also testing. It is our commitment to academic quality and student outcome that has enabled us to become the first private, not-for-profit university for thirty years, and only the second ever.

I hope that you find this history interesting, and become as excited as we are about the next phase of higher education in Regent's Park.

Professor Aldwyn Cooper
VICE CHANCELLOR AND CEO
REGENT'S UNIVERSITY LONDON

Professor Aldwyn Cooper,
Vice Chancellor, wears the robes
especially created for Regent's
University London featuring a
design that pays tribute to Queen
Mary's glorious rose garden in
Regent's Park.

Regent's University London Launch Event

Top: Professor John Drew, University Chancellor (centre), is flanked by Pro-Chancellor Ian Mehrtens (left) and new Honorary Fellow Beth Stroble of Webster University, St Louis (right), while Vice Chancellor Aldwyn Cooper looks on (far left).

Above: Professor Toni Hilton, Dean of the Faculty of Business and Management, congratulates Sir John Gieve, former Deputy Governor of the Bank of England, on his appointment as an Honorary Fellow of Regent's University London.

Top: Professor Judith Ackroyd, Dean of the Faculty of Humanities, Arts and Social Sciences, presents an Honorary Fellowship to Cornelia Meyer, a distinguished expert in the energy field. Chancellor John Drew is on the right.

Above: Professor Judith Ackroyd addresses the audience.

On 29 June 2013 a ceremony was held to install the University's first Chancellor, and to award honorary fellowships. This was followed by a celebration in the grounds.

Professor Cooper (left) shows his approval as Chancellor John Drew invests Professor Beth Stroble with the hood signifying her Honorary Fellowship of Regent's University London.

The University's Directorate and new Honorary Fellows assemble in front of the main entrance.

From left to right: Brian Hipkin (Dean of Students), Sir John Gieve (Honorary Fellow), Cornelia Meyer (Honorary Fellow), Beth Stroble (Honorary Fellow), Ian Mehrtens (Pro-Chancellor),

Professor John Drew (Chancellor), Professor Aldwyn Cooper
(Vice Chancellor), Professor Judith Ackroyd (Dean of HASS),
Sue Shutter (Director of Human Resources), Professor Toni Hilton
(Dean of BaM), Sinéad McQuillan (Company Secretary),
Carl Teigh (Chief Finance Officer).

Celebrations for the new Regent's University London and 100 years
of education in Regent's Park bring together current staff and students,
as well as alumni from Bedford College and many distinguished
international guests. At top right, Professor Aldwyn Cooper joins
the party with his wife, Rosalind.

The event turned out to be a day of sunshine and good cheer.
Lady Sophie Laws, seen at bottom left with her husband, Sir John
Laws, has been a highly valued member of staff at Regent's since
September 1985.

Bedford and Before

Gates donated by Henrietta Busk, a pioneering Bedford College student in the Victorian era, bear a motto that encourages all who enter to live life to the full.

Regent's Park

The story of 100 years of education in Regent's Park begins with the move of Bedford College to the parkland premises in 1912–13. Regent's Park itself had been both forest and farmland. In medieval times, the land was part of Middlesex Forest, and contained deer, boar and wild cattle. The area was situated between the manors of Tyburn and Rugemere, and its parish church was known as 'St Mary's by the bourn' (Tyburn, one of London's many hidden rivers) – hence the name Marylebone. As Ann Saunders writes in her history of Regent's Park, 'For nearly 500 years after the Norman Conquest, the local pigs fed on its acorns, and … the village of Tyburn existed as something quite separate from London Town three miles away'. Following the dissolution of the monasteries in the 1530s, Saunders continues, Henry VIII 'acquired the manor and enclosed a hunting park in the north-east, which he called Marylebone Park' (Ann Saunders, *Regent's Park*, 1981, p. 12).

Charles I mortgaged the park during his reign to raise funds for muskets and gunpowder for the Civil War. Following the war, the Commonwealth government, headed by Oliver Cromwell, seized the park and used as many as 16,000 of its trees to help pay war debts. At the Restoration of the monarchy, Charles II became owner of the park, and chose to use it once again as a hunting chase, which remained its destiny for the next 150 years.

The corner of Regent's Park that is now home to the University was once the site of Marylebone Farm, a house built for Sir William Clarke, who was Cromwell's secretary during the Civil War but then declared loyalty to King Charles on his Restoration, and died in battle in 1666. The farm prospered until it became the largest in the county of Middlesex.

The park also attracted wealthy and mobile Londoners who wished to escape the increasingly crowded and noisy streets of the city. Samuel Pepys noted in his diary on 7 May 1668: 'Then we abroad to Marrowbone, and there walked in the garden; the first time I ever was there, and a pretty place it is.'

This bucolic outpost of London took on a new lease of life in the early nineteenth century, when

Above: Marylebone Farm was constructed in the seventeenth century on the site that now houses the University.

Above, right: A bucolic scene from the nineteenth century, with South Villa in the background. The building was demolished in the early twentieth century to make way for the new buildings of Bedford College.

a lease to the Duke of Portland expired in 1811, and the new Prince Regent (later George IV) saw the potential in the parkland for a glorious new palace and complementary grand villas. George was already known for his interest in style and architecture, and one of his most extravagant commissions, the Royal Pavilion in Brighton, still stands as a monument to his taste for glamour. He appointed a commission to create a park and to let adjoining land on building leases.

In 1818 John Nash, the appointed architect and a friend of the Prince Regent, drew up plans for a vast, rounded park surrounded by palatial terraces, and for a lake, a canal, fifty-six villas and a summer palace for the prince. He envisaged a grand processional route from St James's Palace to the park, along what is now Regent Street and Portland Place. The nineteenth-century diarist Henry Crabb Robinson was very pertinent about the way in which the development would endure into the future: 'this enclosure, with the new street leading to it from Carlton House, will give a sort of glory to the Regent's government, which will be more felt by remote posterity than the victories

of Trafalgar and Waterloo, glorious as these are' (Henry Crabb Robinson, *Diary*, 1872).

The 'double circus' of elegant terraces surrounding the park is still very much in evidence today. Of the fifty-six planned villas, only eight were constructed, owing to the exigencies of the Napoleonic wars diverting too much cash from the royal coffers. Only two villas, St John's Lodge and The Holme, remain from Nash's original conception of the park. The summer palace for the Prince Regent was never built.

The park gradually became the home of various organizations, including the Zoological Society of London (founded in 1826; London Zoo opened in 1828 in the north-east corner of the park) and the Royal Botanic Society (from 1840). It was not until 1835, during the reign of William IV, that members of the general public were allowed into sections of the park, and even then on only two days per week. In the 1930s, after the Royal Botanic Society decided not to renew its lease in the park, the formal rose beds of Queen Mary's Gardens were laid out, thus continuing the royal connection that began with

An early aerial view of Bedford College shows how South Villa was then incorporated into the layout. The Botany Garden in the foreground is now the site of the beautiful Secret Garden at the University.

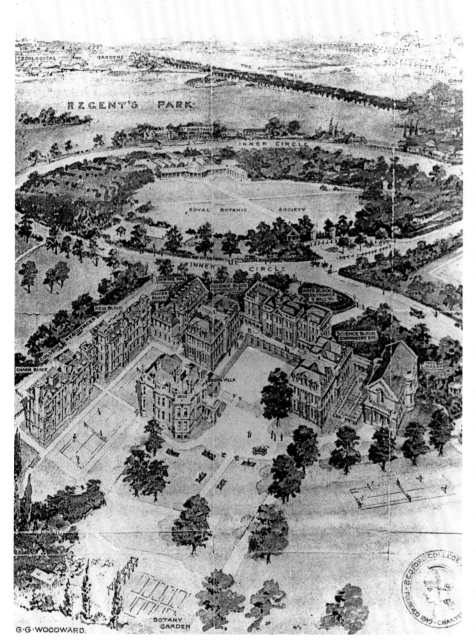

Henry VIII's appropriation of the park 400 years earlier. Today Regent's Park (including Primrose Hill) encompasses 197 hectares (487 acres) and, with its landscaped trees and water and its ducks, geese, herons and squirrels, continues to bring the English countryside into the heart of the city.

South Villa, on the University's current site, was designed and built in 1827 by Decimus Burton, a noted architect who was responsible for many other fine houses as well as the original buildings for London Zoo, some of which are still visible today. His father, James, was a builder who raised much of the initial finance for Nash's grand scheme, and Decimus was only eighteen when he designed The Holme, an elegant villa that adjoins Regent's University, with gardens sweeping down to the lake. The other surviving villa is St John's Lodge, designed by John Raffield and occupied by the Duke of Wellington's elder brother in the early part of the nineteenth century. The hexagonal gatehouse in the University grounds is the only remaining vestige of South Villa, but the location endures, to encircle the current buildings. This is surely the loveliest university setting in England.

Right: The tradition of giving seminars in the grounds has continued to this day, especially in times of hot weather during the Summer School period.

Below: Just over half of the staff of Bedford College pose on the steps of the Tate Library in the mid-1920s.

Life itself, every moment of it, every drop of it, here, this instant, now, in the sun, in Regent's Park, was enough.

Mr Morris, the resident porter, and his wife stand in front of South Lodge, c. 1917. The hexagonal lodge is the only surviving trace of the nineteenth-century South Villa, designed by the renowned architect Decimus Burton, who was also responsible for the original buildings at London Zoo.

Bedford College

Her Majesty Queen Mary officially opened Bedford College on its new site in Regent's Park in July 1913; the ceremony was overseen by the Principal of the College, Margaret Tuke. The brief history contained in this book covers the century from this point until 2013, when Regent's College became Regent's University London (RUL).

The story of 100 years of education in the park may be divided into three chronological sections, and into several thematic parts. The three sections of the chronology are Bedford College (1913–84), Regent's College as a confederation of institutions (1985–2006), and Regent's College as a unitary institution (2006 onwards). The culmination of the last stage is the creation of Regent's University London, in 2013. The thematic parts of the College's history are related to the education of women, the international nature of studies at the College, and the institutional steps undertaken in order to achieve unitary status.

The main pointers for the future of Regent's University London are enshrined in the current

Above: Elizabeth Reid, a founder of Bedford College, was a strong advocate of education for women.

Opposite, top: The original Oliver Dining Hall, where staff and students were served by maids who brought the food from adjacent kitchens.

Opposite, bottom: After the first Oliver Hall was destroyed by bombs during the Second World War, the new refectory provided a more streamlined, modern space, with stylish wall decoration.

strategy documents and the associated documents related to the acquisition in 2012 of Taught Degree Awarding Powers (TDAP). In brief, however, it is clear that the University will retain its international focus and will continue to emphasize its mission to create global leaders for the twenty-first century.

The origins of Bedford College lie in the efforts of a number of people, but particularly Mrs Elizabeth Jesser Reid (later Dame Elizabeth Reid), to advocate and encourage the development of higher education for women. (It is worth noting that the origin of Rockford College, now Rockford University, in Illinois – see the next chapter – was as a college supporting the education of women.) The College was founded in 1849 as the Ladies College and was located at 47 Bedford Square. Before the College made its final relocation to the park, it had an interim move in 1874 to York Place, Baker Street.

Elizabeth Reid's advocacy of education for women arose from a number of motives, including the progressive and philanthropic causes of the Unitarian Church, to which she belonged. In a history of Bedford College, M. Pakenham-Walsh

notes that Mrs Reid dreamed of creating '"a College for women or something like it"', partly to 'save the daughters of the middle and professional classes from the "dreary futility of life" which was their experience in the early part of the 19th century' (in J.M. Crook, ed., *Bedford College*, 2001, p. 15). The College's initial academic offerings included Biblical Teaching (from a strictly non-sectarian point of view), English, Latin, Moral Philosophy, Mathematics, Scientific Geography, Elocution, Vocal Music and Harmony, and Drawing. In its early days, the College suffered from a distinct shortage of women enrolling as students, as well as from financial difficulties and matters of governance. Indeed, throughout its history, Bedford College appears to have struggled with matters of finance and governance. As the following chapters show, these problems have also formed part of the Regent's experience.

In his introduction to the history of Bedford College, J.M. Crook comments that the College 'had never been academically autonomous. Teaching had always been shared on an intercollegiate basis' (*ibid.*, pp. 2–3). The story

Left: The elegant stonework on the Tate Library has an art nouveau style, which was popular in the Edwardian era.

Below: Photographed here in 1952, part of the ground floor of Herringham Hall was used as a Periodicals Room. The Library was subsequently extended and the space reallocated.

Opposite: The magnificent gates to the Queen Mary's Gardens face the main entrance to the University. Queen Mary, wife of George V, was a loyal supporter of Bedford College.

Equality of Education

A key aspect of what has made Regent's successful has been the continuing determination to ensure that women and men are treated equally. This core feature of education may be traced back to the creation of Bedford College, and has been retained throughout the latest developments at Regent's. It is interesting to note that Rockford College (now Rockford University), the creator of Regent's College in the 1980s, had been a pioneer in women's education in the United States, much as Bedford College had been in the United Kingdom. Rockford, based in Illinois, began in 1847 as an educational institution for women called the Rockford Female Seminary; forty-five years later it became Rockford College. Rockford's most famous graduate is the pioneering social worker Jane Addams, one of the earliest women to win a Nobel Prize (the Nobel Peace Prize in 1931).

Regent's University London is now firmly co-educational, and there is an undoubted and undiminished view that women and men are equal partners in the educational enterprise. Opportunities are, and should be, open to all in the differing fields of psychotherapy and counselling, business and management, film and media, international relations, international events, and fashion and design. The leadership of the schools, faculties, departments and programmes has been filled always on the basis of merit, rather than on any discriminatory criteria. This is not only as it should be, but also a true reflection of the heritage and the future of Regent's.

Regent's College must be the most wonderful place
in England to work ... It has trees, water, tranquillity, that
element of surprise as you approach the red-brick pile ...

VICTORIA THOMPSON, FORMER BRITISH THEATRE ASSOCIATION AND
EUROPEAN BUSINESS SCHOOL EMPLOYEE, 2012

A view of the Tuke Building dating from 1930, when it was still in the process of construction.

of Bedford College was always closely linked to the development of the University of London, and Bedford never had 'a monopoly of women's higher education in London, or anything like it' (*ibid.*, p. 3). Nevertheless, it was always clear, right into the 1960s, that Bedford was the leading college in London where women enjoyed the special distinction of being educated within a single-sex context. The first cohort of male undergraduates was admitted in October 1965. This author (male) remembers being at the London School of Economics and Political Science (LSE) in the mid-1960s, when the proportion of women to men at the LSE was 1:7. The prime sources in London for female companions were nursing colleges and Bedford College. This anecdotal comment is confirmed by many of the author's contemporaries, both male and female.

❋

Prior to Bedford College's move to Regent's Park, there had been a lengthy search for new premises as the activities of the College grew and the occupation of the York Place property became more difficult. Finally, a legacy in 1908 from Mr Robert Turle permitted the negotiation of a Crown lease of South Villa and its 3.2 hectares (8 acres) of grounds on the Inner Circle of Regent's Park. The acquisition of the villa and its grounds by Bedford was not welcomed locally. In her history of the park,

Above: An early image of Bedford College, before the additional buildings created an enclosed quadrangle.

Right: A sign above a doorway from the current quadrangle to the Acland Building is testimony to the building's use in Bedford College days.

Bedford College for Women, Regent's Park, N.W. - Library and Tennis Courts.

Above: The Tate Library. The building still looks the same today, although the plane trees are now towering veterans. The tennis courts have long gone, but the indentation in the lawns remains.

Right: A view of temporary classrooms at Bedford College before the Second World War demonstrates clearly why new buildings had to be funded and constructed.

Ann Saunders recounts that 'the residents did not take kindly to the new tenants and protests were staged in the Park' (p. 132). However, the architect Basil Champneys was appointed, and new building began in 1911. M. Pakenham-Walsh reports that the grounds and the villa were occupied as early as 1909 (in Crook, *Bedford College*, 2001, p. 27). South Villa was eventually demolished in 1930, and today the only remaining part of the villa is the small gatehouse, South Lodge, at the entrance to what is known as the Acland car park.

A separate commission from Champneys' work was the Tate Library, designed by Sydney Smith and built by Amy, Lady Tate in memory of her husband, Sir Henry Tate. The building work at the College was completed by 1913, and the official opening was carried out by the royal patron, Queen Mary, on 4 July.

As the twentieth century progressed, Bedford College attempted to remain an independent and fully functioning part of the University of London, to which it had been admitted in 1900. There was an increasing shortage of space on

By 1930 the nineteenth-century South Villa had outlived its usefulness, and it was demolished.

the Regent's Park site and a financial squeeze that eventually, in 1985, forced Bedford into a merger with Royal Holloway College in Egham, Surrey. The nature of this merger soon became apparent as an acquisition in name, even though the academic strength of Bedford may have been considered as greater than that of Royal Holloway. Bedford disappeared from the merged College name in 1992.

A key role in this merger was played by Professor Dorothy Wedderburn (Principal of Bedford College, 1981–85, and of the merged College until 1990), who managed the final stages of the transition from the Regent's Park site, and integrated the academic programmes and administrations of the two colleges to form Royal Holloway and Bedford New College. Her own account of this period, given in a published history of Bedford College, sets the story within the wider context of universities in the United Kingdom. It is evident that the designation of Bedford as one of the 'small' institutions within the University of London meant that a merger would be required 'in order to achieve economies

A dramatic image of devastation, when enemy bombs destroyed the Oliver Hall in May 1941.

REGENT'S COLLEGE

HERRINGHAM BUILDING
REBUILT 1948-50 ON SITE OF ORIGINAL BUILDING
OPENED BY H·M QUEEN MARY IN 1913
DESTROYED BY ENEMY ACTION IN 1941

Robin Oakley

Lecturer in Sociology, Bedford College, 1965–83

Opposite, top left: Queen Elizabeth The Queen Mother converses with staff and students on the last royal visit to Bedford College, in 1984. Note the 1980s hairstyle!

Opposite, top right: The Student Common Room of Bedford College in the late 1960s, when men first came on the scene in equal numbers with women undergraduates.

Opposite, bottom: The front gates to Regent's University are a reminder of the Bedford College years.

The year in which I arrived at Bedford College was the first year in which men were admitted as undergraduates. Our department was housed on the second floor of the Reid Building, and I was aware that until very recently this had been a dormitory for young women. However, apart from the fact there were still some bathrooms that remained unconverted, this history of usage was no longer evident, and from the start my experience of being based in Reid, as in the College generally, was of working within an integrated Bedford College. I remember fondly the spacious Library, with its tall ceiling and huge windows, as the one place in the College where there was an atmosphere of quiet reflection and peaceful learning. Ensuring that the book and periodical collections were adequate for student needs was a mission to which I dedicated myself from early on.

My idyllic image of this setting was shattered one afternoon in the summer of 1982, when an IRA bomb exploded under the bandstand just beyond the car park beside Reid during a military band concert. It was a weekday in late July, so the College was relatively empty, and at the time I was in the Library and registered a loud 'thud'. At first I gave it no attention, but very quickly the word was being whispered that a bomb had exploded by the car park. As my car was parked there, I walked round to investigate. A horrifying sight met my eyes as I peered through the boundary hedge into the park, initially of several motionless bodies of bandsmen in black uniforms laid out just in front of me. Then, around the bandstand, an array of overturned chairs, clothing and belongings, and other varied debris scattered across the lawn area, with several knots of people still gathered around others who had been injured. This sight continues to be one of the most powerful images that remains with me from my time at Bedford.

of scale and a sounder academic base' (in Crook, *Bedford College*, 2001, p. 356). As Crook explains in his introduction, prior to the merger with Royal Holloway, Professor Wedderburn, her Council and members of staff had considered merging with King's College London, University College London or the equally 'small' Westfield College (pp. 7–8). None of these options turned out to be possible, and the linking of Bedford and Royal Holloway became the only solution.

The end of Bedford College in Regent's Park heralded the start of discussions as to what, or who, would occupy the site. Perhaps to the surprise of many, and thanks to the good intentions of the Crown Estate, the decision was taken that the new occupants should continue to be of an educational nature; the final choice was Regent's College, the UK-based charity established by Rockford College in Illinois. There is a certain irony that another 'small' college with its roots in the education of women replaced Bedford on the site. The next stage of our story is the foundation of Regent's College in the mid-1980s.

Enid Light

Last President of the Bedford College Old Students Association, 1952 55

Reid Hall in those days consisted of two wings, Bostock and Shaen, and these were joined by a 'bridge of sighs'.

Although it was seven years since the war, we still had rationing, and we were each allocated a weekly screw of sugar and a lump of butter to take to our rooms for entertaining visitors as we toasted crumpets (not rationed!) over our coal fires. The only heating in our rooms was a coal fire, and we were allowed two scuttles of coal a week. We had a maid to clean the room, make and change the bed, and clean and re-lay the fireplace. The maid on our floor, a Mrs Jones, was very nice, but sadly helped herself to the college linen and finished up in Holloway prison.

All visitors had to be out of our rooms by 10 pm, and if we went out we had to be back in College by 10.30 pm unless we had special dispensations. We had no locks on our room doors, and there we were in the middle of a public park, where any stranger could walk in off the street in the daytime and enter our rooms.

All London University graduands received their degrees in the spring following the examinations, and the ceremony was conducted in the Albert Hall. The Queen Mother was Chancellor of London University and each year dished out literally hundreds of degrees to us all – quite a feat!

The beauty of being at Bedford College was, of course, its situation, in the middle of the Royal Park, with the roar of the lions in the Zoo at night and the lovely chimes of the Abbey National Building on Baker Street in the daytime, to say nothing of the fact that the heart of London was on our doorstep. A campus that is unique. No wonder we were all so sad when we lost it!

Dr Claire Gobbi Daunton
Bedford College, 1971–74

I arrived to study History at Bedford College in 1971. It was beautiful weather in that early October, and I remember being hugely impressed by the buildings and by the friendliness of the people, both fellow students and those who taught us, many of whom I am still in contact with. We divided our time between the main college buildings – I loved the excellent Library, Herringham Hall, the College shop, where we bought our stationery, and the gardens – and St John's Lodge, which housed the History and Classics departments. St John's was very special: a beautiful nineteenth-century villa with gracious rooms, and a very good feel to it. We all miss that. Some of us were fortunate to have accommodation at the north end of the park, in Hanover Lodge, where a number of rooms looked down over Regent's Park. Here we were within walking distance of the main College and Baker Street, and on from there to Oxford Street and the delights of central London. It was a wonderful time in a great place.

Rachel Whittaker, MBE, JP
Bedford College, 1962–65

I spent my final year in a gracious room in Reid Hall where the furniture included a nineteenth-century rosewood bow-fronted chest of drawers. The walk late at night from Baker Street Tube station was deemed 'unsafe', and my boyfriend gave me 2s. 6d. (half a crown) to pay the taxi fare of 1s. 9d. Taxi drivers used to turn their headlights down the 50 yards of the drive and not leave until I was safely through the doors of College.

In 1963–64 I was Vice President of the Student Union, facing a three-cornered battle to be elected. At one of the Union meetings in Herringham, we were invaded by students from the North London Polytechnic, trying to kidnap our 3-foot-high mascot (a wooden goat, symbolizing Candida, the goat we had adopted in Regent's Park Zoo). I recall jumping up from the top table, where the President was trying to calm the meeting, grabbing the mascot and running down the corridors with it. The North London students left empty-handed.

A gathering in front of the main entrance to Bedford College in 1985, in the days just before the merger with Royal Holloway College took place.

Overleaf: A view of South Lodge in early summer. The young tree in the centre of the photograph is one of those used to decorate Westminster Abbey on the occasion of the marriage of Prince William to Catherine Middleton in 2011.

Rockford to Regent's

The Rockford College Era

Set amid rolling countryside about 145 kilometres (90 miles) west of Chicago is the semi-industrial city of Rockford, Illinois. A key feature of the city is Rockford University, a private, independent, co-educational liberal arts college set on a campus of more than 120 hectares (300 acres). The college was founded in 1847 as the Rockford Female Seminary, an educational institution for women. In 1892 the seminary was renamed Rockford College. The college became fully co-educational in 1958, and changed its name to Rockford University in 2013. Rockford's best-known graduate is Jane Addams, who in 1889, with her friend Ellen Gates Starr, created in an underprivileged and impoverished area of Chicago Hull-House, a social settlement and refuge for the poor modelled on Toynbee Hall in London's East End. Addams later became a prominent peace activist, which led to her receiving the Nobel Peace Prize in 1931; she was the first American woman to receive the award.

In spite of the two colleges having similar origins as pioneering institutions for women's

education, Rockford College was the slightly surprising successor to Bedford College on the Regent's Park site. Numerous institutions – commercial, educational and religious – had coveted this prime site and made representations to the Crown Estate. The campus was described by the *Chronicle of Higher Education* as 'one of the

The campus of Rockford College in Illinois, formerly Rockford Female Seminary and now known as Rockford University.

world's choice academic sites, set amid the trees and ornamental gardens of London's Regent's Park' (5 October 1983), and by the *Daily Telegraph* as 'arguably one of the best sites in London for an educational institution' (14 May 1984). A booklet of about 1985 on Regent's College sets out the campus as consisting of 'a dozen ivy-clad buildings enclosing a quadrangle and surrounded by broad lawns, ancient trees, tennis courts and gardens … Within the last few years, the campus has been extensively renovated and modernized to meet current standards and needs … preserving the architectural beauty of the buildings'. For all possible successors to the Crown lease over the College site, one of the great attractions was the magnificence of the location.

Professor Dorothy Wedderburn, Principal of Bedford College at the time, points out in a published history of the College that, as far as Bedford was concerned, 'the sale of the Regent's Park site presented great problems' (in J.M. Crook, ed., *Bedford College*, 2001, p. 371). It is evident that, to their great credit, the Crown Estate Commissioners permitted the leases 'to be

disposed of to educational institutions' only (*ibid.*), and discussions were held with Rockford College via its UK-registered company, Regent's College. The negotiations between these two 'small' colleges appear to have proceeded reasonably well, since there was agreement that those members of Bedford staff who did not wish to move to Egham, Surrey (the site of the merged Royal Holloway and Bedford New College), could be taken on by Regent's. In addition, the arrangement permitted a degree of dual control of the Regent's Park site as Bedford moved out and Rockford/Regent's moved in. Such cooperation even led to the staging of a number of Bedford events at Regent's after Bedford had fully moved to Egham, including the 'Down Memory Lane Reunions' in May and September 1999 as part of the 150th anniversary celebrations (*ibid.*, p. 377). There was also a return to the campus in 2013 for a number of Bedford alumni.

Rockford College took over the lease on the park site in 1984 for twenty-seven years, and founded Regent's College primarily to provide a 'study abroad' programme, with courses that had a

Look what the Old Girls missed

Shando 20/11

WHEN Bedford College, beaten at last by its overdraft, left Regent's Park and trundled off to Egham some of the Old Girls were not pleased.

It was, after all, a most historic and distinguished seat of learning, the first college to award degrees to women and what a marvellous site for a college, right in the middle of Regent's Park, and anyway it was their old college and it had no business moving to Egham.

A few weeks ago, indeed, one of them, Mrs Grace Morris, 75, actually opened a rescue fund to bring it back, starting it off with her own £5 note.

DR NORMAN STEWART, president of Rockford College, Illinois, and his splendid new prize in Regent's Park.

It is already operating. The first 30 students from Rockford are half way through their first London semester, the European Business School, Salford University, the University of Southern California and the Thomson Organisation all have master courses in full flight.

The new rector, James Platt is clearly delighted that everything is going to plan.

"We have turned a small college of London University into a new kind of international higher educational institution," he says. "Already we have 16 nations represented in the hall of residence . . ."

America is and will continue to be the main nation represented there. Rockford hopes that most, if not all of its student body will spend part

---

Above: This cheeky piece of journalism, reporting on the Bedford College move and the establishment of Regent's College, appeared in the London *Evening Standard* on 20 November 1985.

Below: A newspaper advertisement from 1985 for 'part-time British staff' to teach at the new Regent's College.

clearly British focus, such as 'Winston Churchill as Statesman', 'Roman Britain' and 'King Arthur'. The first announcement of courses and recruitment advertisement requested applications to fill the posts of 'part-time British staff'; such express and explicit advertising would not be permissible today. The first students (mostly US sophomores and juniors) arrived the following year, and a steady flow from the United States has continued over the nearly thirty years since then.

REGENT'S COLLEGE

Regent's College, a British educational foundation, is acquiring the Regent's Park site occupied until now by Bedford College of the University of London – among many other activities it will offer a number of courses in 15-week semesters (September-December, January-April) for US sophomore and junior year students.

Part-time British staff are required for the following, to be offered this September:

Government	: Winston Churchill as Statesman
History of Religion	: Christianity in Britain 597-1603
Theatre	: Criticism of Current Productions
Literature	: King Arthur
English Music	: Middle Ages to Handel
Sociology	: The Immigrant Experience in England
Business Administration	: International Business
History	: Roman Britain: An Archaeological & Historical Survey
Economics	: The European Economic Community

Applications should outline experience appropriate to the above themes, and be addressed to Mr James Platt, Rector, Regent's College, Inner Circle, Regent's Park, London NW1 4NS.

Regent's College is a developing institution in the international educational field, open for academics and foundations to suggest courses, research and other projects having a strong international component that might be introduced on a self-funding basis. It will be the home of a number of institutes, administrative services and new forms of higher education cooperation with the USA and other parts of the world.

On 2 September 1985 the first semester began at the new Regent's College, and fourteen courses were offered; one (BA in International Business) is still offered today, and others continue in modified forms. Rockford sent thirty students and some of its own teaching faculty. On the staffing side, a select – or, at any rate, selected – group was recruited: Nicholas Dromgoole, ballet critic of the *Sunday Telegraph*; Louis Halsey, composer and conductor; Roland Quinault, who was beginning his work on the Churchill papers; Boris Rankov, classicist, Oxford oarsman and coach of the Athenian trireme; and Sophie Laws, theologian. The programme was elegantly presided over by Dain Trafton, Academic Director. Wine was served at faculty meetings, and the semester was marked by a procession in academic dress through the gardens, to an amazed audience of squirrels. The *Evening Standard* reported on the chic cream sofas in the front hall and on the lavatories: 'Regent's College now has the finest plumbing that money can buy' (20 November 1985; text with thanks to Sophie Laws).

The Regent's College logo, which attempted to bring the four schools together, c. 1995.

The HE 'Industrial Park'

Following the departure of Bedford College, the Regent's campus had effectively become a higher education industrial park. In addition to Rockford, other institutions took up residence: the European Business School (EBS) moved on to the campus in 1985, widening the international focus with its emphasis on languages and internationalism and its programme of student exchange. The site also welcomed a group of unconnected institutions related to international development and others connected to the theatre (some of these are listed right).

There was also an English language school, the Bell Institute, much later replaced by Internexus (see pages 63–65). Other institutions came and went over time. The School of Psychotherapy and Counselling (now the School of Psychotherapy and Psychology; see pages 60–63) was established in 1990, thus maintaining the presence of the social sciences and applied science on the campus. In 1994 Regent's College agreed with Webster University in St Louis,

Key Institutions on the Campus 1985–97

BELL LANGUAGE INSTITUTE

BRITISH-AMERICAN DRAMA ACADEMY (BADA)

BRITISH THEATRE ASSOCIATION (BTA)

CENTRE FOR WORLD DEVELOPMENT EDUCATION (CWDE)

EUROPEAN BUSINESS SCHOOL LONDON (EBSL)

INTERNATIONAL PLANNED PARENTHOOD FEDERATION (IPPF)

OVERSEAS DEVELOPMENT INSTITUTE (ODI)

REGENT'S BUSINESS SCHOOL (RBS)

ROYAL INSTITUTE OF PUBLIC ADMINISTRATION (RIPA)

SCHOOL OF PSYCHOTHERAPY AND COUNSELLING

A stylish rendition of Regent's College taken from a prospectus in the 1980s.

Missouri, to license and deliver its degrees through the Webster Graduate School and the British American College London.

In 1997 John Payne and his wife Gillian established Regent's Business School (RBS) on the campus. RBS offered full-time three-year undergraduate degrees with strong emphasis on such management streams as Finance and Marketing; these were complementary offerings to those of EBS – but, at times, as we shall see, also competitive.

Since the nature of this history is firmly connected to the development of Regent's College as a unitary institution, it is impossible to explore the manifold and fascinating back stories of each of the institutions on campus at that time. However, it is worth detailing the history of a few: the British Theatre Association, the Centre for World Development Education, and the Overseas Development Institute, all of which either no longer exist or have moved off the campus; and the European Business School, which is still on the site.

BRITISH THEATRE ASSOCIATION

The British Theatre Association (BTA) was founded in 1972 for the encouragement of the art of the theatre, and created a reputable library of works on drama, theatre and the stage. The BTA existed on the Regent's College site until its final year of operation in 1989–90. The BTA can be

André Georgi
European Business School, 2012

Regent's prepared me for an international work atmosphere and allowed me to understand how different people from different backgrounds interact.

Stefano Balestrini
MA Global Management with Pathways, 2010

The whole experience at Regent's was unique. I've made lasting relationships with more than forty people from thirty-five different countries.

Veyza Rodriguez

International Exchange Student (Peru), 2010

This is the best school I have attended, and I have also studied in Arequipa [Peru], Buenos Aires [Argentina], Milan [Italy] and Seoul [South Korea]. Regent's in London was clearly the best. … The school provides plenty of opportunities to grow and to create. In my case, I enjoyed participating in a 'Dragons' Den' and in International Student Bureau activities (for which I organized a business talk with a guest speaker).

The place is just marvellous. It is exactly how you dream a university environment should be, with the location in the park. Inside, the facilities are comfortable, and it's just like being at home.

seen as an interesting precursor of the London School of Film, Media and Performance (LSFMP), founded within the Faculty of Humanities, Arts and Social Sciences (HASS) in 2008–2009, and now known as the Regent's School of Drama, Film and Media.

CENTRE FOR WORLD DEVELOPMENT EDUCATION

The origins of the Centre for World Development Education (CWDE) lie in the coming together in 1965 of eight UK non-governmental organizations concerned with overseas development, initially known as the Voluntary Committee on Overseas Aid and Development (VCOAD). VCOAD became CWDE in 1977, and arrived on site in 1985. The organization's main aim within education was to pioneer the teaching of world development issues in the school curriculum, a subject still of prime importance to Regent's.

CWDE became Worldaware in 1992. It offered the Worldaware Business Awards. Among the presenters of these awards between 1989 and 2004 were HRH The Princess Royal, Chief Emeka

Anyaoku and the politicians Lord Callaghan, Kenneth Clarke, Clare Short and Hilary Benn. It is clear that the period spent at Regent's College was a very profitable and successful time for Worldaware, as its former Director, Derek Walker, comments: 'In my opinion, our time at Regent's College saw the beginning of the most productive period in Worldaware's existence.' Worldaware left the Regent's site in 2001, and was incorporated into SOS Children and Global Eye in 2005.

OVERSEAS DEVELOPMENT INSTITUTE

The Overseas Development Institute (ODI) was based on the Regent's College campus between 1985 and 1996. ODI originally came to the site because it recognized a synergy with other international organizations on the campus; this was an attraction for numerous other original subtenants. The ODI held many conferences, residential courses and meetings on the Regent's campus, and attracted large audiences for many high-profile British and international speakers, including Dr Norman Borlaug, a recipient of the

Nobel Peace Prize, and Chief Emeka Anyoaku, former Secretary-General of the Commonwealth. The ODI is now located in Southwark, south of the Thames.

European Business School

The European Business School is important as being the first private institution in the United Kingdom to take on the difficult task of offering a full-cost, fee-paying undergraduate-level business course entirely outside the state system. The higher education landscape in the 1970s and early 1980s was one that was still dominated by the public sector, with only the University of Buckingham being incorporated in 1983 as a private university (having been a university college since the early 1970s), strongly supported by the Conservative government of Margaret Thatcher.

The history of the European Business School in the United Kingdom is complex, and this account is necessarily brief. The acronym EBS has been used in the UK since 1972. The companies using the name have changed ownership and corporate names (as we shall see below), and this history will use EBS or European Business School to cover any and all of these differences.

In the early 1970s what came to be known as the European Business School took shape in France, Germany and the UK. It grew out of an initiative by Philippe Guilhaume to expand the Institut d'Economie et Coopération Européenne (IECE), which he had created in Paris in 1967. Through connections in Germany and the UK, what began initially as an institute for French students became a European project with centres in several major cities. The IECE established the first EBS programme at its Paris centre on rue de la Paix with a four-year post-Baccalauréat course. The course incorporated the study of business and two foreign languages with a third year spent abroad combining academic studies and internships. This basic structure became the model for subsequent EBS centres.

To service the year abroad, EBS Paris established companies in Germany through Prof. Dr Klaus Evard, known as EBS Frankfurt (although it was originally located in Offenbach),

Francis Prosser

European Business School, 1988

I have some very fond memories of both the School and the life around it. At the time it was quite a new thing for the UK – the combination of business with the European cultural outlook – and exciting, despite the intensity of the work rate, the demands of work experience and study abroad. The School was pioneering and, as students, we also felt a bit like pioneers. The early facilities were sadly in spirit with that, though.

and in the United Kingdom. The European Business School (London) Ltd was established in 1972 with a French controlling interest (51% IECE; 26% Guilhaume, with Ian Goatman and David Evans; minority British interest 23%). The 'year abroad' courses for students at EBS Paris (and later EBS Frankfurt) were delivered at the Centre of Economics and Political Studies (CEPS) at Queens Gardens, Bayswater, directed by Goatman; the organization later moved to teaching premises in Chandos Place, near Covent Garden.

In 1975 Peter Coen, already teaching at EBS and also a lecturer in Marketing at the Polytechnic of Central London (now the University of Westminster), was appointed as Director of EBS London; from 1976 the London shareholdings were also taken on by Coen. He was the key creator and founder of EBS in the UK, taking on all the entrepreneurial responsibilities of a new institution, establishing the School in its own right, and fighting to ensure its academic and commercial independence. From the mid-1970s, the courses were delivered from premises rented from City University (more specifically, those of the City

University Business School, now the Cass Business School) at Lionel Denny House on Goswell Road in Clerkenwell. EBS London thereby had access to teaching rooms, a library, catering facilities and other central services, thus providing the necessary basis for its operation. The City University arrangement gave EBS a considerable degree of credibility and allowed it, in the typically British phrase, to 'punch above its weight'.

As the number of students attending from France and Germany grew each semester, the number of regular visiting staff also grew: for example, Gerald Shaw taught Economics, and Sam Ward, Law. By 1979–80, in addition to Coen, EBS London had a full-time academic staff of three: Greg Spiro (Head of English), Paul Bullock (later Head of Business Studies) and Nick Bowen (later Head of Languages). This small team was joined by a number of other regular part-time members of staff who made significant contributions, including Frank Siegmund and George Igler (who later became full-time staff), N.D. Quy, Terence Godwin and George Jones. During the first fifteen years of EBS London, the academic staff were supported

Former Prime Minister Edward Heath at the official opening of the European Business School at Regent's College in 1987. Regent's University's first Chancellor, John Drew, stands second from right.

by such outstanding administrators as Annette Hales, Terry Davies, Adèle Mallinson, Lesley Nixon and Nicole McGlone.

By 1979 EBS London was ready to recruit its own students for the four-year EBS Diploma programme. Legally, a new company, the European Business School (UK) Ltd, replaced the European Business School (London) Ltd. The shareholders of the new company were Coen (50%), Evard, Director of EBS Frankfurt (25%), and EBS Paris (25%), which was represented on the board by its directors, successively Philippe Magnen, Patrick Gouverneur and Jean Mauduit. The Managing Director of EBS in the UK remained Coen, who attracted over time a number of senior advisers, such as Professors David Liston, Nigel Reeves and George Wedell, and Michael Shanks, Peter Waine, and Anthony Frodsham (who chaired the EBS Advisory Council in the 1980s). The part-time and small complement of full-time staff taught both the visiting students and the first small annual intakes of UK-registered students. Since undergraduate education was free to state university students in the United Kingdom until

Max Fraser
European Business School, 2007

I was, and still am, very pleased that I found EBS. I remember my time there very fondly, and I am constantly reminded of how well taught I was, and simply how much I derived from being there for three years. It is a very well put-together programme, and one that I've always felt bettered the offerings of universities that my friends attended across the country, mainly owing to the rigour of the course. The demands were not too high, but were far greater than those demanded of students at Leeds, Manchester, Bristol, Edinburgh, Newcastle, etc. This more structured and disciplined approach worked very well for me. It was a huge luxury to be among so many representatives of other nations and cultures, and I really felt that EBS made the most of those differences in order to foster an ability to work within a team. ... I am sure that many of my fellow students at EBS will go on to do great things.

Back to school: Sir Leon Brittan delivers his warning from the EBS lectern yesterday

Brittan says EMS discipline needed to conquer inflation

By Colin Narbrough

Sir Leon Brittan, the Euro- the benefit would be to world trading system, not an
pean Commission Vice-Presi- Britain. attempt to pull up the

Timo Scheiber

BA International Business and Management Studies, 2004

I am still in touch with former classmates from all over the world, and we meet up whenever one of us happens to be in town … this is what I call a truly global network.

Mohd Feezul Abdul Bakar

MA Global Management with Pathways, 2009

I got more than I bargained for! A practical learning environment, small class sizes, an international collegiate atmosphere and a magnificent location.

The distinguished Conservative politician Sir Leon Brittan gives a speech at EBS in May 1990.

the twenty-first century, with maintenance grants widely available, the EBS initiative of offering a fee-paying programme in business studies with languages was exceptionally brave.

Throughout its early existence, EBS London faced the typical challenges of a small, growing enterprise: it had to ensure its independence and freedom of manoeuvre; cope with financial difficulties, especially short-term cash-flow issues; balance academic principles with the necessities of economic survival; and carve out an independent and identifiable niche within the higher education market. In the field of European business studies, EBS London had to keep developing in order to compete with the then giants, such as the BAEBA (BA in European Business Administration) programme at Middlesex, the French schools supported by Chambers of Commerce, and the range of Europe-wide collaborative courses run in the UK by many polytechnics. Many of these challenges facing the young enterprise were later also faced by Regent's College as a whole.

The main programme offered by EBS was the four-year undergraduate Diploma in European

Business Administration, in practice 'validated' by the success of its graduates in meeting the needs of business, and formally certified by the combined Academic Boards of EBS London, Paris and Frankfurt. Each Diploma certificate was counter-signed by the directors of the three schools.

The structure of the programme was broadly as set out originally by EBS Paris, namely two years of study in London, including both French and German languages, one year of study abroad – spent equally in semesters at EBS Paris and EBS Schloss Reichartshausen (as Frankfurt had become) – and a final year back in London. This mirrored the programme run by the other two schools. Those familiar with the main existing (2013) EBS undergraduate programme – BA (Hons) International Business – will see that it is still structured in this way, but it is now three and a half years, and with a choice of nine foreign languages.

EBS relocated to Regent's College on its formation in 1985 and became one of the first large founding institutions of the campus community. It considered external validation

Early graduates of EBS London; this photograph dates from 1994.

following the successful and steady growth in student registrations, from ten first-year students in 1980 to seventy in 1986. Initially EBS took out a sublease for a part of the Tuke Building. Over the door into Tuke from the Acland car park, it is still just possible to detect the outline of the words 'European Business School EBS at Regent's College was formally opened on 7th May 1987 by Edward Heath (former Prime Minister of the UK, 1970–74)'.

In 1988–89 serious tensions arose within the EBS group of interconnected schools. For EBS at Regent's College, these tensions were particularly associated with the need for additional capital investment and the introduction of the proponents and eventual owners and operators of a new EBS in Italy, Stefano and Elio D'Anna. The end result was the break-up of the group into two camps, one led by EBS Paris and EBS Madrid, the other coalesced around EBS in London and Schloss Reichartshausen. Within EBS London, there arose internal opposition to the Director and the emergence of a Parents' Committee; the outcome was the acquisition of shares and control by

John Payne, who had risen to be Chair of the Parents' Committee.

A period of both rivalry and intermittent discussion between the two opposing groups followed. After 1996 this was largely resolved, with positive and active collaboration between the European Business Schools in Paris, Madrid and London. Attempts have been made in recent years to establish a united brand as EBS International (EBSI). However, despite the continuing strength of EBS Paris and the growing strength of EBS Madrid, the schools within the network operate independently but collaboratively.

From the early 1990s, the story of EBS at Regent's College London became increasingly linked with the development of Regent's College itself. Originally this interconnection arose from the strategic and operational moves within the College of the EBS shareholder John Payne, his wife, Gillian, and their wider family, to extend their interests to the control of the College as a whole. Later this link between EBS London and the College became a crucial issue arising from the need to establish a properly governed

Some of the first students to attend the new Regent's Business School, in 1997.

and financed educational charity that would be acceptable to the UK's Charity Commission. Once EBS London was thus registered, it was able to expand its offerings into short courses in business and languages and into the postgraduate field, and to extend its undergraduate degrees into cognate fields. Although it had long been the intention of EBS London to have a wider portfolio of programmes and courses, the financial, operational and legal difficulties of the early years meant that such moves were not feasible until the late 1990s.

As of 2013, the position of EBS London is that, while it is no longer a separate financial or legal entity from Regent's College, it preserves a key brand of the College, offering two undergraduate and four postgraduate degrees. It is also a significant contributor to the College's bottom line, with about 1000 students, two-thirds of them on the undergraduate programmes of International Business (about 600) and International Events Management (about seventy). EBS London is regarded as a premier brand for the College within the UK and internationally for practically orientated business programmes.

Development of Regent's College

The early years of the twenty-first century witnessed several key stages in the development of Regent's College. In essence, the main step was to ensure that the campus community would become a single entity. The principal drivers behind this desire and need to develop into a unified College were:

the requirement for systems of Quality Assurance

the bringing together of all the programmes and schools into a broadly single system

the ultimate ambition of achieving university title and status

the obtainment of Taught Degree Awarding Powers (TDAP) as a stepping stone towards this ultimate ambition

the securement of the lease and the development of the property

the establishment of sound finances

Developing Quality Assurance and Enhancement

One of the key steps towards College unity
and university title has been the development
of a system of Quality Assurance (QA) and
Enhancement (QE) – together known as QAE – as
an integral part of the academic and institutional
framework. The initial move towards this
system was the development within each of the
individually validated schools on the campus of
their own version of a QA or QAE system. In most
cases, this was in response to the demands of their
validators, whether the Open University Validation
Services (OUVS), City University or the University
of Wales.

The QAE system that was developed within
the European Business School London arose from
the experience of a number of Quality Circles that
were set up by the Academic Director, Professor
Eric de la Croix. From the staff reactions to these
Quality Circles, progress was made towards
'establishing a culture of Quality Enhancement'.
The intent of the original QE developments was
to devise and implement a system that gave real

benefits to both students and staff – a system that
positively encouraged everybody to assess what
they do, to introduce changes where improvements
were needed, and to ensure that changes made
had real quality impact on the students. Above all,
it was noted that the system of quality should be a
means to an end and not an end in itself.

Parts of the QAE system developed within
EBS were adapted and re-engineered by Regent's
Business School for its own purposes and, once
the schools within the College came together,
the best of these QAE principles, processes,
procedures and practices were combined with the
experience of the School of Psychotherapy and
Counselling Psychology (SPCP) via the University
of Wales to create the QAE system of the unitary
institution. This system was developed by the
College's Academic Registrar, Steven Quigley, and
eventually his team within the Academic Registry.

A view of the Tuke Building in winter snow shows the dramatic shape of one of the 'Great Trees of London' – the Regent's University plane (centre).

The Senate's Quality Audit Committee took on the appropriate powers of supervising and overseeing the QAE systems and operations, and has further developed these functions within the University's Senate.

Moving Towards the Campus as a Single Entity

Over time there was a gradual acceptance of the view that the College had to become a single academic and commercial unit. Only through this achievement could there be real strength and control. To this end, it was considered essential that all programmes operating within different schools should follow a similar format and purpose. This movement towards unity embraced both the establishment of common central services supporting academic work – such as information technology, library and learning resources, internships and placements – and student services, as well as common systems for Quality Assurance and eventually, in 2013, the development of a new Regent's academic model by a team led by Professor Judith Ackroyd.

As far back as 1997, there were voices that acknowledged the need for such unity across the campus. At the time of the establishment of RBS, Marcel van Miert, Director of EBS London, noted:

It is the overall strength of the campus achieved through the individual strength of each school that makes Regent's College a success. It is this campus-wide approach of providing the right education for the right student with the right services that allows us to satisfy demand from undergraduates, graduates and employers. ... Regent's College focuses on offering clear choices to potential students and [tries] to accommodate them, taking account of an individual's strengths, their abilities and aspirations whilst always seeking to serve long-term future goals to the best of our ability.

(EBS LONDON NEWSLETTER, AUGUST 1997)

Within the general move towards becoming a unitary institution, there were a number of major tensions relating to governance, finance and structure. Any student of organizations will recognize that these themes are not unusual; indeed, they are almost inherent in the progress and growth of any institution.

Noelle Reno
BA Media Communications, 2006

As an American, the first time I visited Regent's I was totally besotted: Queen Mary's Gardens, the ponds, trees, lamp posts, flower pots, brick exterior, etc. I had to attend a university in London, and there is absolutely, hands down, nothing that compares to the look and feel of Regent's.

My parents were so pleased that I would be able to experience the classic university-type environment by attending Regent's. It really felt like a campus in a rural town, but with the best of London on the doorstep.

For these reasons, Regent's draws a wide range of students, so it's a fantastic place to grow as a person. There are some impeccable contacts one can make at Regent's, and for many this is a major bonus of attendance. It was for me; networking is so key in my business as a model and fashion entrepreneur!

Regent's Business School

One of the key tensions that arose within the schools of the College was a direct consequence of the difficulties arising over the 'ownership' and 'direction' of the College, which in turn could be partially attributed to the stressful antagonism between the two main business schools on the campus, EBS and RBS. The Regent's Business School, a private, for-profit institution owned by John and Gillian Payne, had grown out of the success of the existing EBS organization and programmes, and had then begun to outgrow these origins as it established itself with significant programmes in its own right. RBS was set up and launched with the successful validation of its three-year BA degrees in June 1997.

Following the initial leadership of Dr Edwin Kerr, the academic direction of RBS was taken on by Dr Richard Gregson, originally the Director of Modular Degrees at EBS. Gregson's considerable contribution to the success of RBS should be acknowledged as he, and its commercial and administrative staff and directors, managed to

negotiate this tough period. Gregson was a great 'ideas man' with, as Dr Tommie Anderson-Jaquest, former Head of the Department of Management, Business and Human Resources, comments, a 'willingness to delegate responsibility and to give autonomy [to others] to develop and plan appropriate actions, so long as activities were carried out in the best interests of the School'.

The essential characteristic of the programmes offered by RBS was that they gave a detailed and intensive focus to the key functional streams within the business studies discipline. The three-year degrees concentrated on global business and management with depth and strength in the management areas of finance, marketing and design. As in the case of the EBS degree programmes, the RBS degrees were validated by the Open University Validation Services. They were applauded for their focus and concentration, and were clearly differentiated by having no requirements for language study, semesters abroad (apart from a Gateway option to study for a semester at a partner institution) or work placements. In fact, as a natural outcome of

Another illustration from an early Regent's College brochure, designed to attract American students. In this image, the Tate Library appears to echo the buildings of an Ivy League campus.

endeavouring to be ready for the world of work, RBS students undertook voluntary internships.

In the summer of 2005, hostilities increased markedly between the Trustees of Regent's College and Gillian Payne, then President of RBS. Announcements were made that RBS would leave the campus premises and move to a new site at Imperial Wharf, and that services that had been previously shared within the College would henceforth be administered by designated RBS staff members. Webster University was also initially persuaded to join RBS in its move to Chelsea.

Staff and students were invited to see the newly built site at Imperial Wharf, and considerable money was spent on attractive marketing materials. However, according to Tommie Anderson-Jaquest, support for the new venture was lacking. Webster University realized that the facilities provided at Chelsea would be substantially fewer than those at the idyllic Regent's Park site, to the detriment of students, and so withdrew its support. This period of uncertainty lasted throughout the second part of 2005 and the first few months of 2006. For staff members below directorate level, no further word

was received about the progress made towards the move. Consequently, in anticipation that the move would take place in the summer of 2006, as originally planned, teaching and administrative activities continued as usual. However, on 6 March 2006, without warning, staff and students were informed that Regent's College had acquired RBS.

The most difficult part of the transition rested in the hostility towards RBS staff members after the acquisition. Resentment was voiced most strongly by the College's central services departments and by senior academic managers within EBS. As a consequence of the enormous challenges faced in attempting to reintegrate all of RBS's business functions, friction was particularly visible in marketing, admissions and finance. As regards the latter, EBS staff members hoped to eliminate RBS completely, because the School's reintegration posed a threat to EBS London's competitive edge in respect of student recruitment.

Throughout the rest of 2006 and into 2007, academic staff members in both schools fought a war of attrition via papers, recommendations and threats in response to the College Trustees' decision that RBS could remain an independent entity but would have to become a Management School. As a condition, it was mandated that the RBS International Business programmes be withdrawn to avoid competing with EBS's long-established international offering. In addition, RBS staff were advised that new programmes would have to be designed, developed and validated by OUVS very quickly. Negative pressures took a heavy toll on RBS staff members in 2006.

The loss of RBS's well-established programmes, coupled with the task of developing new ones at short notice, presented real challenges in the spring and summer of 2006. At that time only a few academic staff members were full-time, and resources were severely limited. Today RBS staff and students are to be commended for having established a clearly identified set of business programmes and, by 2012–13, for having become the largest and financially strongest part of the Faculty of Business and Management (BaM). The careful design and pioneering features of the RBS degree programmes are a credit to the relevant people within the BaM Faculty.

The most significant change that needed to be effected was the transition of RBS from the control of Gillian Payne, which was exercised through two trust boards with more or less identical trustees and a number of management companies, to a system of governance that was fully acceptable to the Charity Commission. This transformation was brought about through a series of delicate manoeuvres in 2005–2007 under the skilful chairmanship of Eric de la Croix. The main objective was to 'clean up' the governance structure so that it was no longer an obstacle to the larger target of seeking Taught Degree Awarding Powers.

The appointment of new Trustees eventually enabled the governance of the College to be satisfactorily resolved, and led to the unification of the different schools and other legal entities on the Regent's campus. There were still several key matters that needed to be sorted out, including mediation between Mrs Payne and the College to settle any issues of compensation from her to the charity; the resolution of a large VAT liability arising from previous arrangements between the Payne companies and so-called 'charitable

trusts'; and the establishment of a new College
trust that would take over all the obligations and
responsibilities for running Regent's.

With the exception of negotiations with HMRC
relating to VAT liability, which took two more years
to agree, the other complex matters were resolved
by late 2006 through intensive work by the
Chair of the Board of Trustees, the Acting CEO,
Professor Michael Scriven, and other members
of the College, including other Trustees. Some
delays to the creation of a forward-looking and
unified College resulted from a further period
with interim chief executives, changes to the
chairmanship of the Board of Trustees, and some
resistance to the merging of all constituent entities
on the campus, especially EBS London, into
the single Regent's College Educational Trust.
It was not until a new Chief Executive, Professor
Aldwyn Cooper, took up his position at the start
of 2007 that the College could really take
appropriate measures to develop strategies for
capital expenditure, integrated approaches to
human resource management, and plans for
academic development.

School of Psychotherapy and Counselling Psychology

The School of Psychotherapy and Counselling
emerged in the late 1980s in order to consolidate
the teaching provision of a Masters in Psychology
of Therapy and Counselling being delivered in
London by Antioch University in the United States
under the directorship of Emmy van Deurzen.
The School was formally established in 1990 and
developed in the 1990s, providing a range of
courses that addressed the growing independent
profession of counselling and psychotherapy in
the United Kingdom. In this period a team of
experienced and well-educated counsellors and
therapists assembled on the Regent's College
campus to deliver Diploma, Masters and Doctoral
programmes that gained validation from City
University in London. At the same time, members
of the School also played important roles in
developing the governance of the burgeoning
professional bodies of the British Association of
Counselling (BAC; now the British Association for
Counselling and Psychotherapy) and the United

The first reunion of alumni from the School of Psychotherapy and Psychology was held in 2013.

Kingdom Council for Psychotherapy (UKCP). Van Deurzen was elected the first Chair of the UKCP on its foundation in 1993; indeed, she ensured that this embryonic beginning for the profession had a base at Regent's College for the first two years of its life. During the same period the School became a recognized training and accrediting member organization of the UKCP, and remains an active member to this day, hosting the UKCP's research conference in 2012 and 2013.

Leading a number of like-minded colleagues, Van Deurzen (by this time a professor) developed a uniquely British approach to existential psychotherapy that has become world-renowned. In 1988 she founded the Society for Existential Analysis, which has since developed and attracted considerable interest and respect from both within the United Kingdom and internationally. Members of the academic staff of the School have continued to play a crucial role in the management and development of the Society, and the School continues to provide qualifying Diplomas, Masters and Doctoral programmes for existential psychotherapists.

In 1996 Van Deurzen left Regent's College, and Professor Ernesto Spinelli became Head of School. During this time the School transferred validation of its degrees to the University of Wales and launched a new professional Doctorate in Counselling Psychology to meet the British Psychological Society's (BPS) requirement for counselling psychologists to be qualified at Doctoral level. Also during this period a highly successful Foundation Certificate in Counselling and Psychotherapy was developed, aimed at introducing counselling skills and principles to a wide range of the caring professions; in addition, it formed a pre-qualifying course for the growing Masters degree in Psychotherapy and Counselling.

In 1998, as the UKCP extended its training requirements, additional advanced Diplomas in Integrative Psychotherapy and Existential Psychotherapy were added to the School's programmes for trainees wishing to register with the UKCP and practise professionally. Since this time the School has become well known for its distinctive existential and pluralistic ethos, for which it is now internationally recognized.

Internexus students visit Stonehenge in 2013. Cultural visits are a vital aspect of their studies.

Another significant development around the start of the twenty-first century was the introduction of a professional course in Mediation and Alternative Dispute Resolution. Developed by one of the School's Senior Fellows and well-known existentialist, Dr Freddie Strasser, and a prominent legal expert in the field, Paul Randolph, the course has established the School as a leading exponent of psychological approaches to mediation. Now led by Randolph, the course has been attended by a large number of international and UK legal dignitaries, and has provided training to the legal professions and to such organizations as the Tutu Foundation.

As Regent's College began to integrate the many schools on its campus into a single higher education institution, in 2006 the School was renamed the School of Psychotherapy and Counselling Psychology, in deference to the growth of its counselling psychology programme. Under the leadership of Dr Maria Luca and, from November 2009, Dr John Nuttall (now Professor), the School became a prominent part of the College's new Faculty of Humanities, Arts and

Social Sciences (HASS), under the aegis of which in 2011 it successfully introduced Foundation and BSc programmes in Psychology. The BSc obtained BPS accreditation in 2012, and the course is unique in its capacity to draw on expertise from all areas of the School and Faculty in the teaching of social and counselling aspects of psychology. The School plans to introduce a range of Masters degrees in different psychology disciplines over the next few years. Notwithstanding this, the School's international reputation as a trainer of psychotherapists remains high and, under the patronage of the new Regent's University London as of May 2013, all the School's taught programmes are expected to become internally validated Regent's University awards. At this time, the School was renamed the Regent's School of Psychotherapy and Psychology in recognition of the increased contribution of psychology and counselling psychology to its curriculum.

Throughout the period of integration into the University, the School has maintained a strong research ethos, with approximately 100 Doctoral students on its register in 2013

A stylized view of the main entrance to the University also shows its proximity to the stunning Queen Mary's Gardens opposite.

and a high proportion of its staff holding Doctoral qualifications. In 2012 a new professional Doctorate in Existential-Phenomenological Counselling Psychology was introduced, gaining accreditation from both the BPS and the Health and Care Professions Council. In deference to the School's clinical training ethos, all its clinical training staff are highly qualified and experienced professional practitioners, able to bring their clinical knowledge and research to bear on their teaching. This experience, coupled with the learning resources provided by being part of a larger faculty and university, gives the School a unique training environment, whatever the level at which students wish to study or staff wish to teach.

Many of the School's current staff, former deans and the present Head of School are graduates. Others graduates have gone on to make valuable contributions in the areas of academia and clinical practice.

Internexus

Regent's University has its own English Language School on campus. The School teaches hundreds of students annually, and the study period ranges between two and forty-eight weeks. The English Language School has not always been owned by Regent's; its origins are to be found in the United States, with links to Rockford College.

In 1981 the company Excellence In Education was founded in the United States, with the aim of establishing a series of English language study centres. The first centre was established in January the following year, at a private, not-for-profit college in Utah. In May 1987, having visited a study centre in Maryland and being impressed by its operations, the President of Rockford College in Illinois approached Excellence In Education with a view to setting up a similar centre on his campus.

In August 1994 Excellence In Education and Yázigi International, a Brazilian chain of language schools, formed a joint company named Internexus. The goal of the joint venture

Michael Collins knows the University inside out. He is now Deputy Maintenance Manager, but started as an electrician in 1996, when, as he remembers, 'It was touch and go if the College would survive.' Much was in urgent need of repair at the time, notably South Lodge, which was just a shell and, as a listed building, proved expensive to bring back to standard. The Maintenance Manager of that era wanted to repair it as cheaply as possible, but fortunately, as Mick recalls, 'The Crown Estates weren't having any', and it is now a showpiece for the original design by Decimus Burton. Mick has been impressed by the overall improvement in the appearance of the grounds and buildings since then, and is excited by the prospect of the new acquisitions. As he pragmatically states, 'The more money they spend on the place, the better it gets for the students, and I get to keep my job.'

was to establish a global network of centres of international education in order to provide opportunities for language and multicultural training throughout the world.

In January 1995 Jim Gunn, a faculty member of Rockford College and the Dean at Regent's, asked Internexus to set up one of its schools in London, on the Regent's College campus. Later that year Internexus English Language School started at Regent's with two classrooms and fewer than thirty students. Almost twenty years later, and after four successful British Council inspections, a management buy-out, and the takeover in 2008 by Regent's College, the School now teaches in excess of 600 students annually, many of whom progress on to the degree programmes at Regent's University London.

The School offers not only English Language programmes but also a rich and varied social programme for its students. Since many of the students are on campus for less than four weeks, it is essential that they sample all that London and the United Kingdom have to offer; this is a vital part of their study programme and adds to

Opposite: The brilliant leaves of Virginia creeper ablaze on the Tuke Building in early autumn.

Overleaf: The quad provides an ideal setting for students to mingle and take a break between seminars.

their overall experience in London. Teachers take the students to a different pub every Thursday, visit museums and street markets, and in the summer months organize day trips to other cities and destinations with cultural value. The School also runs a successful Pearson test centre on campus, and in 2012 examined more than 600 students. It prepares students for the Cambridge International English Language Teaching System (IELTS) exam, and has high progress and pass rates and excellent success rates with students going on to higher education studies.

Several of the English Language students come from South Korea, where Internexus has an office in the Gangnam district of Seoul that has excellent partnerships with prestigious Korean universities. These universities send their students to Regent's University for an increasingly popular study and internship programme that forges links with many local companies. The School, however, has an excellent balance of nationalities, and receives students from all over the world; in fact, it has contacts in every country that sends students to study abroad.

The School's management works very closely with English UK, which is the world's leading language-teaching association, with more than 450 members. It uses this relationship to establish connections with state governments worldwide, and has welcomed many students from these governments in recent years.

The year 2013 marks another year of progress for the School, as it merges with the Department of Languages and Cross-Cultural Studies from the Faculty of Business and Management, to form the new Regent's Institute of Languages and Culture. The Institute will continue to offer language provision to Regent's students while researching new areas of degree specialisms in the language and culture disciplines. These degrees will then be taught by the Institute as Regent's University degrees.

Consolidating the College

A New Team

A review of the College's operations in light of the problems of governance that it had faced led to the establishment of a new corporate structure. With advice from the Charity Commission, this new structure was formalized by amendments to the Regent's College memorandum and articles of association on 27 May 2005, and formally came into practice in June 2006.

The new single charity, merging Regent's College and the European Business School Educational Trust, was constituted as a company limited by guarantee under the Charities Act. This led to a requirement for a new Trustee Board and the appointment of a single Chief Executive.

The initial Board was chaired by Professor Eric de la Croix, who before retirement had been Academic Director of the European Business School (EBS), and two Trustees nominated by the Charity Commission. In addition to Regent's College and EBS, the new charity and its Board took responsibility for a number of other schools, including the Regent's Business School, the School of Psychotherapy and Counselling Psychology, the British American College London and the Webster Graduate School. At that time there were still a number of other organizations that continued to lease space on the campus.

Over the next two years, Professor de la Croix strengthened the Trustee Board with the recruitment of experienced people who could help to build the new organization and improve its governance. These included John Ormerod (later Chair of the Board of Trustees), Barry Sterndale-Bennett, Raj Pradhan (formerly Vice Chair of London South Bank University) and Professor Roger King (a higher education consultant and formerly Vice Chancellor of the University of Lincoln). Successive phases of recruitment to the present day have continued to strengthen the Board and broaden its expertise.

While the search took place for a permanent Chief Executive, a number of people took on interim or short-term roles. These included Professor Michael Scriven (Director of EBS),

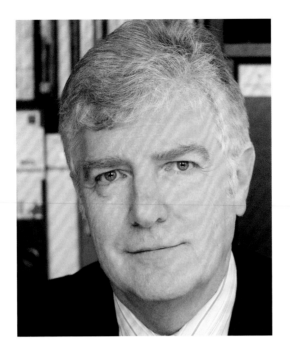

Martin Timbrell, first Dean of the Faculty of Business and Management (BaM); Professor Judith Ackroyd, current Dean of the Faculty of Humanities, Arts and Social Sciences (HASS).

David Morgan (Director of the British American College), Peter Douglas (a member of the Trustee Board) and Professor Leo Murray (formerly Director of the Cranfield School of Management). After an extensive search, Professor Aldwyn Cooper, Pro-Vice-Chancellor at the University of Glamorgan was appointed as Chief Executive, and took up the post full-time in January 2007.

At that point, although the overall charity maintained the campus and provided a range of shared services, the individual schools retained a high degree of autonomy. This led to duplication of operations in many areas and a less than fully efficient operation both academically and commercially.

The first tasks for the new Chief Executive were to review the organizational structure, rationalize the academic provision, ensure that all staff and students enjoyed the same excellent experience, further develop the academic standards, and plan for the acquisition of degree-awarding powers (an objective set by the new Trustee Board).

The new organizational structure approved by the Board was focused operationally around the

provision of centralized services and academically around the formation of two faculties: the Faculty of Business and Management (BaM) and the Faculty of Humanities, Arts and Social Sciences (HASS). A priority was to strengthen the group of experienced managers already at Regent's by recruiting further members for a strong Directorate team who shared the vision for the College and could unite around the goal of achieving Taught Degree Awarding Powers (TDAP). Two members of the Directorate team were already at Regent's: Truda Turner (previously the Regent's Company Secretary) took on the task of managing the College services and estates development; Spencer Coles, as Head of ExRel, assumed responsibility for marketing, communications, student recruitment, admissions, international partnerships, careers services and alumni.

The existing Directorate members were then supplemented during the following year by the appointment of two faculty deans: Martin Timbrell (formerly Dean of Business at the University of Hertfordshire) for BaM, and Dr Judith Ackroyd (now Professor; formerly Associate Dean of Arts

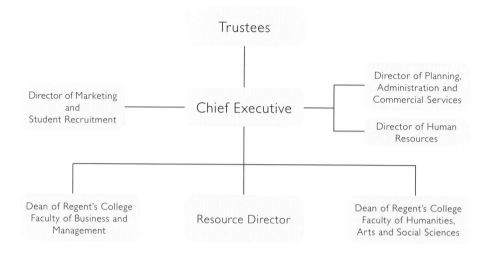

```
                              Trustees
                                 │
                                 │                ┌─── Director of Planning,
                                 │                │    Administration and
   Director of Marketing         │                │    Commercial Services
        and          ───── Chief Executive ──────┤
   Student Recruitment           │                │    Director of Human
                                 │                └─── Resources
            ┌────────────────────┼────────────────────┐
            │                    │                    │
   Dean of Regent's College   Resource Director   Dean of Regent's College
   Faculty of Business and                         Faculty of Humanities,
        Management                                 Arts and Social Sciences
```

at the University of Northampton) for HASS. The vital role of Finance Director was taken on by Roger Cottam, and the crucial role of Human Resources Director by Sue Shutter.

In addition to the academic provision, which did not use the campus space fully, Regent's ran a conferencing business that made a substantial contribution to the College's financial sustainability.

A New Strategic Plan

Higher education institutions that do not have their own degree-awarding powers require validation of their programmes from a validating university that does have such powers. In January 2007 British degree programmes at Regent's were validated predominantly by the Open University Validation Services (OUVS), with the remainder validated either by the University of Wales or, in a small number cases, by City University. The American programmes were all licensed from Webster University, a long-term partner. The OUVS and/or the British Accreditation Council (BAC) had individually accredited some of the

schools. However, the establishment of the new organization as a single institution made it necessary to have a unified accreditation relationship that applied to everybody at Regent's.

The OUVS deferred the individual school accreditation inspections but required an early full institutional review. The first challenge was to produce an integrated strategic plan and a five-year business plan within three months, before the end of the first quarter of 2007. In order to set this in train, a number of principles were established. The first was that the strategic plan should be structured around the plans for the two faculties, followed by strategies in each support area to help achieve these plans. The second was to use all accreditation processes as rehearsals for an eventual application for degree-awarding powers. This meant that each exercise would be built around the preparation of a Critical Self-Analysis (CSA) document structured by the degree powers criteria specified by the Quality Assurance Agency for Higher Education (QAA).

In October 2006, before taking up his post, the new Chief Executive had participated in a two-day

The Mission

Regent's College seeks to foster Internationalism and Professionalism through the provision of appropriate, applied, academic programmes that embody a spirit of international understanding and mutual cooperation, allied to high-level professional capability and responsibility. The primary ambition of the College is to provide a uniquely stimulating, multicultural and plurilingual learning environment in which students aspire to become global citizens capable of contributing effectively and responsibly to a twenty-first-century environment.

The Core Values

EMPLOYABILITY

EXCELLENCE

INTERNATIONALISM

MULTIDISCIPLINARITY

ENTREPRENEURSHIP

DIVERSITY

VALUE-ADDED FOR STUDENTS

GOOD CITIZENSHIP

✿

Originally agreed in March 2006

The College Vision

To become an exemplar of a successful, private, charitable university college, reflected through its attainment of Taught Degree Awarding Powers

✿

To focus on the needs of its students, and to provide the best learning experience and career prospects

✿

To maintain, celebrate and build the diversity of its staff and student base in order to enrich the learning and collegiate experience of all

✿

To establish a strong, clear, unified brand reflecting its values, history, location and aspirations

✿

To be well managed and governed through a strong, efficiently structured, professional management team with effective oversight provided by a board of dedicated Trustees

✿

To provide a first-rate learning environment that develops, extends and makes most effective use of its outstanding campus in central London, and which is developed to provide leading-edge learning methods, facilities, resources and assessment methodology

✿

To have a strong system of academic quality

✿

To contribute to the public benefit

✿

To rationalize, strengthen and build its portfolio of programmes to meet the expectations of its students, their sponsors and potential employers

To grow its student body by 100 per cent across six years, to become a destination of choice for learners worldwide and to establish itself as a selecting rather than a recruiting institution

✿

To reduce the reliance on conferencing as the space becomes required for the core academic business

✿

To reclaim the campus from other organizations, and either acquire them where relevant or discontinue their leases

✿

To be respected by employers, governments, professional bodies and regulators worldwide

✿

To enhance its international reputation both by building further its network of partnerships worldwide and through the profile that the College will develop for the scholarship of its staff, the abilities of its graduates and the importance of the events that it organizes

✿

To become an aspirational employer for staff through its commitment to scholarship, personal career development, equal opportunities, diversity and the provision of a stimulating and excellent working environment

✿

To build a collegiate culture where all staff take interest in the work of others, recognize and celebrate success, participate fully in the College's academic, cultural and social activities, and engage with alumni worldwide

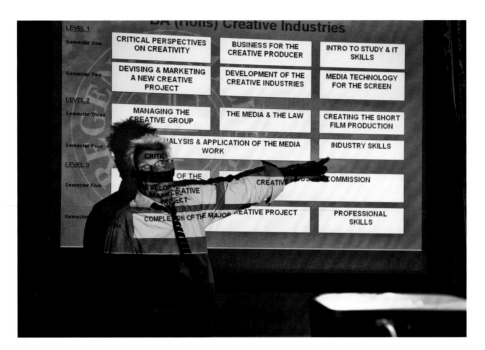

BA (Hons) Creative Industries

LEVEL 1			
Semester One	CRITICAL PERSPECTIVES ON CREATIVITY	BUSINESS FOR THE CREATIVE PRODUCER	INTRO TO STUDY & IT SKILLS
Semester Two	DEVISING & MARKETING A NEW CREATIVE PROJECT	DEVELOPMENT OF THE CREATIVE INDUSTRIES	MEDIA TECHNOLOGY FOR THE SCREEN
LEVEL 2			
Semester Three	MANAGING THE CREATIVE GROUP	THE MEDIA & THE LAW	CREATING THE SHORT FILM PRODUCTION
Semester Four	ANALYSIS & APPLICATION OF THE MEDIA WORK		INDUSTRY SKILLS
LEVEL 3			
Semester Five	OF THE CREATIVE PROJECT	CREATIVE COMMISSION	
Semester	COMPLETION OF THE MAJOR CREATIVE PROJECT		PROFESSIONAL SKILLS

David Hanson, Head of School, emphasizes the practical in a lecture to Drama, Film and Media students.

Board strategy meeting. At this meeting the Board debated revisions to the mission, values and vision of the new College; these are outlined on pages 72–73.

The strategic plan, backed by a five-year financial projection, was approved by the Trustee Board in November 2007.

There was no doubt that the plan was ambitious and controversial. While not everybody necessarily bought into all the elements and implications of the strategy, an overwhelming majority accepted and welcomed its main outlines and details. This support was reported at a number of the regular 'town hall' meetings (as evidenced by the surveys of staff conducted by an independent and professional company) and at the annual Staff Conference. The clear direction and acceptance of the strategy led inexorably to the successful steps on the path towards TDAP and university title.

The continuing review and development of the different iterations of the College's strategy document and the supporting strategies within the faculties and the central services were key to the success of Regent's. The overall strategy established

the clear framework for all members of staff and other stakeholders, including students, to share in the mission, values and vision of Regent's. The implementation of the strategy was discussed in various forums, ranging from Trustees, Directorate and Senate to visiting/part-time and full-time members of staff and to the teams of support staff, whether gardens and estates or careers and business relations.

There were those who felt that the projected growth in student numbers and total revenue was unattainable. Others felt that the academic reorganization would be counterproductive and detrimental to student outcomes. However, these concerns have not been borne out: the growth, sustainability and academic outcomes have met their targets in an increasingly difficult higher education environment, and Regent's has achieved its university status well ahead of schedule.

Among the key developments that followed from this strategy were the finalization of the College Senate and the reorganization of the centralized alumni and careers operations. The creation of the College Senate in 2006 had been

foreshadowed at earlier phases of the development of Regent's, perhaps most notably in the Kerr Report of 1994. This report, compiled by Dr Edwin Kerr (a former Director of RBS, who died early in 2012), called for the establishment of a single academic body within the campus in order to prepare for 'institutional validation for the College as a whole'.

In his report, Kerr stressed that, in order to create the wholeness of the College, 'structural changes are essential'. His major proposed change was 'the establishment in due course of a new body which will be the principal academic body in the College'. He recommended that this body follow usual academic practice and be called the 'Senate of Regent's College'. Behind Kerr's drive for the goal of 'wholeness' was his understanding that 'at present the academic staff largely contribute to the well-being of only one school and see themselves as members of the school rather than of the College as a whole. In future they will also have to see themselves as members of the College who consider and contribute to its well-being as a whole.'

In the subsequent pages of the report, Kerr set out the essential elements of the Senate and its probable terms of reference. These included the establishment of committees with appropriate membership to advise the Senate, including 'a committee concerned with the maintenance and improvement of academic standards and performance'. Kerr also was aware of the propensity of committees to multiply, and two of his principles were:

The number of committees must be kept to the irreducible minimum. They must be established only when they have a real task to perform.

The membership of each committee should be as small as is consistent with the committee being able to deal authoritatively with its terms of reference.

Ultimately, the Kerr Report was ahead of its time, and it was another decade before the College was ready to establish an overall academic

Ian Mehrtens, appointed Chair of the Board of Trustees in 2010 (top); Professor Michael Scriven, former Director of EBS.

institutional body. Much of the groundwork for the College Senate that was then established was laid by Professor Michael Scriven, who undertook a comprehensive review of the institutional academic structure of Regent's before he retired in 2010. The Senate has now operated for several years, and has proved to be one of the essential elements pulling together the academic side of the College community.

Above all, both Aldwyn Cooper and Ian Mehrtens (appointed as Chair of the Board of Trustees in 2010) point to the importance of the crucial relationship between the Directorate and the Trustees in agreeing and implementing the new strategy.

Among the objectives for the new Regent's College was a desire to ensure that all students and staff were treated equally. For students, this meant that they should all be provided with access to the same facilities, resources and support. For staff, it meant instilling a value of mutual respect among all staff and ensuring that there was a coherent pay system that rewarded everybody appropriately and equitably for their contributions. It was clear

that quite different approaches had been taken in different schools.

For students, the first step was to open up to everyone access to learning resources on an equal basis. This required centralizing responsibility for these resources and making substantial additional investment in the Library, IT systems and student services operations. Academically, it meant reviewing the student–staff ratios, contact hours and staffing across the institution. Aspirations were set in place that students would receive on average twenty contact hours per week, that class sizes would be kept small, and that the student–staff ratio would not exceed fifteen to one. It was also agreed that an average 75 per cent of teaching should be delivered by permanent staff on full-time or high fractional (greater than 60 per cent) contracts. The remaining 25 per cent would always be delivered by 'qualified practitioners' either who brought specialist areas of knowledge or who were still actively engaged in relevant employment and could bring current knowledge to inform students.

The Trustee Board had become aware that there was an inequitable pay system in place:

different schools applied different pay scales; academic staff were treated differently from professional support staff; and there existed no clear development or progression system. Benefits at the College did not meet the norms in the higher education sector or even better private-sector employers generally.

Regent's established for all staff a new and more generous pay system, based on the Hay grading system, resulting in increases for most staff that exceeded the national increases at the time. Since that time Regent's has increased average pay by 3 per cent each year, again a figure that exceeds the sector average. Steps were also taken to improve general benefits, including setting an academic base load of 500 teaching hours per year, against the national agreement for full-time staff of 550 hours. Leave was increased to a total of forty-three days per year. Sickness benefits were substantially increased. Pension contributions were increased by up to 10 per cent of salary, and many other benefits were introduced. Further advancements have been made in recent years, and the beginning of 2013 witnessed the initiation of

REGENT'S COLLEGE
LONDON

REGENT'S BUSINESS
SCHOOL LONDON

REGENT'S COLLEGE
CONFERENCE CENTRE

SCHOOL OF
PSYCHOTHERAPY
& COUNSELLING
PSYCHOLOGY

WEBSTER GRADUATE
SCHOOL LONDON

EUROPEAN BUSINESS
SCHOOL LONDON

REGENT'S AMERICAN
COLLEGE LONDON

LONDON SCHOOL OF
FILM, MEDIA & PERFORMANCE

The schools of Regent's College, c. 2009.

an innovative pay system that improves promotion and career progression.

In order to develop the College and integrate all elements, a document called 'Regent's People' was produced. The aim of the document was to ensure that everybody understood the mission, values and vision of the College, and their own place in achieving the strategic objectives. It set out the expectations that Regent's has of everyone and the specific expectations of academics, professional services staff, students, graduates and partners. These expectations indicate a number of attributes that should be shared by all Regent's people, namely that they should be:

Student-focused

Quality-driven

Market-facing

Service-orientated

Professional

Ethical

Charitable

Collegiate

'Regent's People' is a dynamic document that has continued to be reviewed constantly. It has changed year by year as Regent's has developed, and is a work of reference for all staff on institutional structure and cultures.

Union membership has never been strong at Regent's, and the Board and Directorate have never felt that national bargaining would be to the benefit of the institution or its staff, who have gained better provision than the sector as a whole. However, the importance of consultation and the engagement of staff in policy- and decision-making is recognized. Therefore, after a consultation process with all staff, a Joint Consultative Committee of elected representatives of all areas of employment was established, and meets regularly to advise on key policies and developments.

As a single institution, Regent's College needed to develop a new visual representation of the College and its schools in order to show that they were part of the same structure. A number of new approaches were agreed by the Board in May 2007 and were in use until Regent's became

a full university in June 2013, when a revised structure and visual image were unveiled.

An aspiration that stems from the strategic plan of 2007 has been to deliver a five-star academic provision and a five-star environment. Since 2006 the entry standards for students have risen year on year. The number of academic qualifications and research publications, and the level of scholarly activity and engagement with the higher education sector have also risen each year and are now substantially higher than in many universities in the state-funded sector. The physical resources and the quality of teaching, student and circulation space had been allowed to deteriorate. During the last five years a substantial investment has been made in reversing these dilapidations, and today the University environment and facilities better most British universities. The quality of food and beverage provision and on-site accommodation had also slipped below the level expected by the College's students – a concern that the College began to address in 2007. Food at Regent's is now varied and provided through a variety of locations, including the Refectory, the Brasserie/Wine Bar, the Deli, the Coffee Shops and the student Bar and Grill. It is generally agreed to be the best provision at any university in London and beyond. The student accommodation in Reid Hall and the Oliver Flats has also undergone total renovation.

With all the rapid change, it became essential to strengthen internal communications for staff, students, alumni and potential learners. An award-winning new website was developed; an intranet, supported by weekly staff and student e-newsletters, was put in place; and the Regent's magazine *Inner Circle* was launched, as were regular newsletters for alumni. The Chief Executive began to produce a blog. He holds quarterly 'town hall' meetings to discuss key issues with staff, and also holds student 'town hall' meetings to debate major changes. Social media has become an important element in communication, particularly among students, and the communications team has developed its use through discussion with students about their preferences.

Professor Aldwyn Cooper, former Principal of Regent's College and now Vice Chancellor of Regent's University London, pictured in his office.

The New Regent's College

Since it became a unitary organization, Regent's has witnessed further crucial years of development. Professor Aldwyn Cooper, the newly appointed Chief Executive (later named additionally as Principal and now Vice Chancellor), was attracted to the international nature of the College, and viewed Regent's as 'a sleeping giant'. The clear brief from the Trustee Board to Cooper was twofold: to form the College into a coherent whole, and to achieve Taught Degree Awarding Powers (TDAP) as soon as feasibly possible.

Although the College had become a single corporate body by June 2006, it was evident that no proper attention had been paid to what this really meant. There was no single strategic plan. It was apparent that people were not talking to one another across the Regent's College campus and the international network. Cooper tells the anecdote of the president of a US affiliate college being unaware that Regent's had any business school, when, in fact, there were effectively four.

An important innovation in preparing to apply for TDAP was the appointment of a Project Manager for College Development. This job was taken up in November 2009 by Kate Stoneman. Her role was to set out the key steps that needed to be taken and to ensure that all parts of the College sang from the same hymn sheet. Stoneman also helped to bring a more collegiate feel to Regent's College, to improve the consistency of the student experience across the College and to develop a clear understanding among staff and students of what the College was doing, why it was doing it, and why the timing was crucial.

A further area of concern and action for the College was that a higher quality of senior management was required, and there needed to be improvements to the quality of academic staff in general. Without moderating the College's focus on teaching and learning, it was essential to introduce a greater emphasis on attracting academic members of staff with more extensive research track records.

Below: David Hanson, Head of the
School of Drama, Film and Media,
lectures in Herringham Hall.

Bottom: Anna Sullivan, a course
leader in the same school, in a
University classroom.

Partnership with the Open University and the University of Wales

Regent's has had validating relationships with three universities – the Open University, the University of Wales and City University. However, the dominant relationship has been with the Open University through its validation service, OUVS (now part of the Open University Centre for Inclusion and Collaborative Partnerships).

The OUVS pursues a partnership approach to support institutions in maintaining the required quality standards for their programmes, and is particularly helpful in preparing institutions that seek to gain their own degree-awarding powers. The system provides a partnership agreement for institutions that meet the rigorous criteria the OUVS lays down. As an institution demonstrates more experience and commitment, OUVS delegates further autonomy to the institution, such as the ability to nominate and approve its own external examiners. This is helpful preparation for obtaining degree-awarding power.

Following the acquisition of the American InterContinental University London in 2013, Regent's established a new School of Fashion and Design.

The OUVS also facilitates discussion among all its partners in order to share best practice within the UK and internationally. Regent's has been an enthusiastic supporter of the partnership network, and has attended and made presentations at many conferences and seminars.

The OUVS understood the College's ambitions to gain TDAP and eventually university title, and was fully supportive throughout the process. Regent's benefited from the wholehearted assistance and advice of Dr Kate Clarke, the OUVS Director during the period, and the partnership managers, particularly Dr Lynne Orton, who helped the College to reach its current university title. Further, in general, the validation panels normally adopted a partnership approach to assist Regent's in ensuring that all its programmes met the required standards.

Originally, the OUVS felt unable to validate the Masters, taught Doctoral and PhD awards in the School of Psychotherapy and Counselling, so these were validated by City University. When City felt that there was a conflict of interest

with its own programmes, validating powers were transferred to the University of Wales. As Regent's moved towards its own degree powers, it sought to rationalize its validators and moved all taught programmes to the Open University.

Having gained TDAP, from 20 May 2013 Regent's University moved to a position of validating all its own taught programmes, and all students graduating after this date from one of these programmes shall be awarded a Regent's University London degree – a move that has been warmly welcomed by students. However, the University does not yet have Research Degree Awarding Powers, and requires such degrees to be validated by another university. During 2013, Regent's is seeking to become an Accredited Research Centre of the Open University for such awards, and thus to maintain its long relationship with the OU.

All American programmes offered at Regent's are licensed from its long-term partner Webster University of St Louis, Missouri. A new agreement without time limit was approved for these programmes in July 2012. Regent's

now intends to recognize and validate the Webster programmes for a UK degree, so that students shall be able to gain both a Webster and a Regent's degree at the end of their study. However, there are some programme areas not offered by Webster, including Fashion and Design (a new school at Regent's), and discussions are taking place with a prestigious American university with an international reputation in this field to provide US validation for these programmes. In the longer term, while Regent's expects to maintain its current US validation partnerships, it is proceeding towards gaining its own American accreditation from one of the regional Higher Learning Commissions, and hopes to complete this process by 2015. This would make Regent's unique in British higher education.

Faculty of Business and Management

Business- and management-related subjects have always been at the heart of Regent's. Although a decreasing proportion, it is still the case that approximately two-thirds of students are taking specific business-related programmes or are enrolled on degrees with a business major of some kind.

In early 2007 Regent's had four separate groups of academic staff teaching business and management subjects in the European Business School, the Regent's Business School, the Webster Graduate School and the renamed Regent's American College London (formerly the British American College). This led to duplication of skills and knowledge, and a failure both to share best-practice scholarship and research and to use the most appropriate academics across the institution as a whole.

The new Faculty of Business and Management (BaM) was established under its first Dean, Martin Timbrell. The Faculty was organized into four subject departments: Accounting, Finance and Economics; Management and Human Resources; Marketing and Strategy; and Languages and Cross-Cultural Studies. All staff with common areas of interest were grouped into one of the departments. Staff

Students listen intently during a seminar.

were expected to teach across the BaM Faculty on relevant programmes, and to provide service teaching to relevant programmes in the Faculty of Humanities, Arts and Social Sciences. Each department was led by a Head of Department, who would work with the relevant programme directors in each school in order to allocate the best and most relevant staff. Initially this reorganization met with a measure of resistance, but its benefits have been easy to observe.

The two schools in BaM, the European Business School (EBS) and the Regent's Business School (RBS), have different origins and programmes, and attract a different demographic of students. EBS focuses strongly on the development of European business in the global environment. Students on undergraduate programmes at EBS must learn one or two new languages to a level of fluency, and must spend two semesters studying or working in a country where that language (or languages) is spoken. EBS learners spend their Study Period Abroad (SPA) at one of Regent's partner institutions around the world (see list, pages 122–23), which

number more than 150 and therefore provide a large choice for students. Because students at these partner institutions come to Regent's, there is a truly international atmosphere on campus. The language and cultural programmes offered are French, German, Italian, Spanish, Portuguese, Russian, Mandarin Chinese, Arabic and Japanese. The Department of Languages and Cross-Cultural Studies has been the recipient of the Threlford Memorial Cup, which the Chartered Institute of Linguists awards annually, in memory of its founder, to the UK individual or institution that has striven most effectively to 'foster the study of languages'.

In the Faculty there are students of more than 140 nationalities. The largest number of students in EBS come from European countries – from the European Union and Russia and the old Soviet bloc. Owing to the period of study abroad, EBS programmes take three and a half or four years. The language skills developed by EBS students, their ability to work internationally and the global perspective that they gain from their fellow learners make them very attractive to companies

operating in the international market, and their employability is very high.

Undergraduate programmes in RBS cover many of the same topic areas as EBS, but from a more global perspective. Although students in RBS can take languages and study abroad, few at present take up this option (although it is hoped to increase participation in future). RBS programmes appeal more to students from the Middle East, the Indian Subcontinent, China, Asia in general, America and Africa. Many of the students in RBS already speak a variety of languages, and their employability is also high.

Both schools also offer a variety of generalist and specialist Masters programmes in areas as varied as Oil and Gas Trade Management, Global Banking and Finance, and Luxury Brand Management. The Faculty intends to develop this specialist portfolio further and to start offering both taught Doctorate and PhD programmes in 2014.

In 2008 Regent's acquired the respected Internexus English Language School, which had been resident on the campus since the 1990s.

The School was brought into the BaM Faculty to sit alongside the Department of Languages and Cross-Cultural Studies. Its function has been to provide Foundation programmes in order to raise students' abilities in written and spoken English before they commence degree programmes, and to support non-native English speakers throughout their study if necessary. The School also offers a variety of English as a Foreign Language (EFL) and English for Speakers of Other Languages (ESO) programmes to international students to help long-term employment or study elsewhere.

Languages have always been a core area of study at Regent's. In June 2013, in recognition of the importance of language development, both Internexus and the Department of Languages and Cross-Cultural Studies were moved from BaM into the new Regent's Institute of Languages and Culture, a change that will raise their profile, aid the provision across all schools and allow additional specialist short courses and degrees to be established.

After helping to prepare the BaM Faculty for gaining TDAP, Martin Timbrell retired in 2012.

Ann Ridley (formerly Dean of Business and Law at the University of Portsmouth) acted as interim for six months and started the reorganization of the Faculty in order to meet the challenges of further academic improvement and self-regulation. Professor Toni Hilton was appointed as Dean in the spring of 2012. Building on her links with the Association of Business Schools (ABS), she has focused on further programme development, the strengthening of the departments, planning for external accreditations through the Association of MBAs (AMBA) and the EPAS and EQUIS accreditation from the European Foundation for Management Development (EFMD), and on enhancing the Faculty's research reputation.

Going forward, the undergraduate portfolio aims to transform young adults into global business leaders. The University wants its graduates to think and behave as independent, capable, ethical and responsible professional business practitioners regardless of global location or the type of business organization to which they choose to make contributions. The undergraduate focus is therefore on generalist business programmes.

Where there is specialization, it is in industry sectors to which our student body is drawn, such as Event Management. At postgraduate level, the Faculty seeks to develop a range of specialist Masters designed to help students obtain junior- and middle-management roles in growing industries with global reach.

Many students enter family businesses upon completion of their studies. Regent's therefore seeks to emphasize the acquisition of knowledge and skills relevant to this behaviour, such as entrepreneurship and, given the type of business that many of our students' families own, luxury brand management.

The Regent's College Model
United Nations team, 2008.

Faculty of Humanities, Arts and Social Sciences

The arrival of Professor Aldwyn Cooper brought to the campus the establishment of a coherent academic structure comprising two faculties with shared, united central services. The smaller faculty was Humanities, Arts and Social Sciences (HASS). Dr Judith Ackroyd (now Professor), appointed as its first Dean, started in January 2008 and remains in post. Ackroyd was recruited from the University of Northampton, where she had been Associate Dean (Research and Development) in a large School of Arts.

The new HASS Faculty comprised a broad range of subjects when it was established, and is now even broader. Initially, HASS included the School of Psychotherapy and Counselling Psychology (SPCP); Regent's American College London (RACL), with staff from a vast array of subject areas from classics and literature to politics, media and finance; and Webster Graduate School, delivering Masters degrees in Media Communications and Business Studies. There were

Acting students bring a classical piece of Spanish theatre to life in a dynamic workshop performance.

three members of staff who had full-time contracts, and every other member of academic staff was hourly paid. Despite their employment status, the staff were completely committed, enthusiastic, student-centred and, for the most part, open to new developments and challenges.

In 2008 Dr Maria Luca replaced Professor Ernesto Spinelli as Head of SPCP. The School has led on research and is, to date, still the only school on campus to offer PhDs. Luca initiated the very significant step to develop Psychology, now a key part of the School. As her research activity developed, she moved on to become the Faculty's first Research Fellow. In November 2009 Dr John Nuttall (now Professor) took on the role of Head of SPCP, establishing the School as an integrated player in the Faculty and College community.

Lady Sophie Laws was in charge of RACL when the new Faculty was created, having been employed at Regent's since 1985. Laws was, and remains, passionate about her students and the opportunities provided to them by a broad-based US degree. An inspiring and engaging teacher, she sees London as the extended classroom. She has

also had a long commitment to the care of Study Abroad students, and was appointed Director of Study Abroad and Programme Director for Humanities in 2008.

Dr Valerie Kaneko-Lucas was appointed Head of RACL in 2008, bringing experience of working in the US and UK systems, and particular expertise in drama. However, she gradually felt that her interests and strengths might be better engaged within the developing London School of Film, Media and Performance (LSFMP). David Parrish had been Webster University Director for London at Regent's since 2005. He brought the two partners closer during this period and managed to wear the 'two hats' very successfully indeed, threatening one with the other hat when he perceived the need. Parrish and Laws worked very closely together and fostered a most collaborative spirit that eased their schools into the new academic structure positively and seamlessly. They opened their arms to the new staff appointments and institutional ambitions, and sought to see advantages and opportunities for students and staff.

Parrish retired from his leadership role in 2010, but he continues to teach his cherished students. His retirement and Kaneko-Lucas's move to LSFMP coincided with the arrival of Professor William (Bill) Lynch, Webster University's new Resident Director, and provided the opportunity for a re-think on the structure of the two schools. As Webster Director, Lynch took over the leadership of both schools. His new role reduced repetition of meetings and administration between the two schools involving many of the same staff, and effected a tightening of the Webster requirements for the programmes. Lynch very quickly became part of the team (while remaining a Webster employee) and achieved much in this time, particularly on student advising and Webster processes.

In the summer of 2012 Webster and Regent's renewed their partnership agreement, which included a new role for Lynch as Director, Webster University Programmes. In November 2012 Professor Lawrence Phillips took on the role of Head of RACL, which includes both undergraduate and postgraduate programmes.

He and Lynch collaborate very closely and are now working towards Regent's validation of Webster programmes to achieve dual awards.

The appointment of David Hanson, BAFTA award-winning screenwriter, led to the birth of the exciting and innovative London School of Film, Media and Performance (now Regent's School of Drama, Film and Media) and the development of a fresh portfolio of practice-based, industry-linked programmes. In 2013, when Regent's acquired the American InterContinental University London, the HASS Faculty was delighted to gain a new school: Regent's School of Fashion and Design. An ambitious, aspirational academic leader, Gill Stark, was appointed as the first Head of School.

Professor Mark Allinson was appointed as Associate Dean (Academic) in 2008, and had to roll his sleeves up at once. He led the development of ten programme validations in two years, while developing a coherent learning teaching strategy. Allinson and Ackroyd quickly identified distinctive responsibilities that have been effectively managed through a very close working relationship. Allinson, too, is still in post.

Left: The environmentalist Jonathon Porritt (centre) delivered the Jean Monnet Memorial Lecture at Regent's in 2010.

Below: The veteran Labour politician Tony Benn holds an audience in thrall with his anecdotes as part of the 'Speakers in the Park' series in 2008.

In 2013 the Faculty grew from three schools to four, with possible further expansion into a fifth school, Law, in the future. The number of permanent staff on full-time or high fractional contracts, now contributing 75 per cent of teaching hours, has grown from three in 2008 to more than 100. However, the visiting lecturers, who bring current practice into the programmes, are still valued highly. Increased student numbers and better management mean that the Faculty now achieves its full targeted contribution to the central costs. It celebrates growing staff research, and has two established research centres. The subject areas are too numerous to mention. Suffice to say, lawyers, philosophers, international relations experts, film-makers, actors, therapists, coaches, psychologists and many more rub shoulders. For good reason HASS had been described as the 'Balkans of Higher Education'. But from this hotchpotch of areas huddling together in one faculty, an exciting fusion is evolving, and the crossovers are energizing for staff and students alike. The team and the students are enjoying the journey.

International Focus

Regent's prides itself on being the most
internationally focused university in Britain, and
this has always been at the heart of the institution's
entire mission. Regent's has the most culturally
diverse student body of any British university.
It has been a strength of the institution for more
than twenty-five years. There are more than
140 nationalities on campus. Eighty-five per cent of
students come from outside the United Kingdom,
with 50 per cent coming from outside Europe.
While many American students from Regent's US
affiliates' network visit the University for a semester
of study abroad, there are no large concentrations
from any one country among the 4000 degree-
seeking students.

Globally, Regent's has relationships with
more than 150 institutions. Those with which the
University exchanges students and staff are termed
Partners, and those that send students to Regent's
for study abroad are called Affiliates (see the list
on pages 122–23). Increasingly this distinction is
becoming eroded as the relationships strengthen.

The team in the International Partnerships Office
(IPO), led by Maria Veiga-Sánchez, manages
the network pro-actively. This team works with
institutions to develop relationships. Before an
agreement is reached, each potential partner or
affiliate is visited by members of the team to assess
academic quality, consistency of programmes
and the available resources. Regular visits are
maintained by University staff throughout the
relationships.

The IPO team thoroughly briefs students
before they depart on a Study Period Abroad, and
evaluates their experiences and achievements on
their return. Students visiting the University are
also given a full induction on their arrival and are
supported throughout their stay. Regent's is an
active participant in the Erasmus scheme, which
promotes student mobility and enables higher
education students to study or work abroad as part
of their degree, and staff to teach or train in thirty-
three European countries.

To promote further international
understanding, Regent's participates each year
in the Model United Nations competition in

Students at Regent's are able to participate in a wide variety of sports, either just for fun or fitness, or to a high level. The University's polo teams have won many awards.

New York. The Regent's Head of International Relations, Yossi Mekelberg, supported by his assistant Sabrina White, prepares the team. The team of around fifteen students, often from as many nationalities, must immerse themselves in understanding the economy, culture and interests of a country that they are allocated. In recent years, the Regent's team has represented countries as diverse as Togo, Latvia and the Cape Verde islands. In 2013 the team presented Cuba in the debates in the General Assembly and the Congo in the Security Council. They

Sukhwinder 'Danny' Singh
Webster Graduate School, 2004

My days at Regent's College were the days of young aspirations and poignant dreams.

won the award for best position paper in each against high-level competition from elite universities around the world.

Each year the University organizes a conference for all its partners and affiliates. This has grown from a one-day event attended by around twenty delegates into a major function, with over 100 international delegates from more than twenty countries attending in January 2013. The conference attracts eminent keynote speakers and encourages contributions from partners and affiliates. During the three days, delegates have the opportunity to learn about international developments and best practice, and to form their own international networks. In future it is expected that the conference will be opened up to delegates who are not yet part of the Regent's network.

The University's strategic plans include the prospect of establishing campuses outside the United Kingdom, either independently or in partnership with members of the Regent's network. In order to develop the global perspective further, Regent's is also starting to

establish with other universities dual-validated programmes that will be able to be taken by students spending study periods at a number of global locations.

Alumni Development

Until 2008 there was no comprehensive alumni association for former students of Regent's College. This did not stop many alumni, especially those of the European Business School, self-organizing, with the support of the College, reunions and collaborations all over the world. Community, shared values and the ability to professionally associate and network are a way of life for Regent's diverse alumni population. Over the past five years the University has invested in, planned and delivered a supportive community, which means that the extended family of former students retain their links not only with their peers but also with the institution too. Today, Regent's University London Alumni Association is an exclusive club with a diverse and vibrant membership. Regent's alumni are found in over 120 countries worldwide.

All over the world Regent's alumni are now working together to create an inspiring community. They are enriching social and professional life for one another, and supporting Regent's in many ways. This community is nurtured by the alumni team through advancing opportunities for networking, socializing, career development and supporting the University in diverse ways, such as being mentors and student recruitment advocates. The chance for former students to play a new role in the community could start, for example, with dropping into a regular Regent's Club event in London or, internationally, helping to organize a reunion or becoming an alumni mentor.

Regent's alumni now engage with the institution in many ways, and there are strong benefits to membership of this community. Invitations to such exclusive alumni events as reunion dinners and sporting engagements (including regular golfing and football tournaments played against current students), and the growing programme of lectures and seminars form the core of our alumni events programme.

Team-building activities at the annual Staff Conference in 2012.

Free alumni publications and a monthly e-bulletin including exclusive special offers from the alumni community, and a strong social media presence across Facebook, LinkedIn and Twitter, ensure that Regent's alumni stay informed and can participate in a global conversation.

The international alumni network extends across the world, delivering the alumni association locally through organized chapters known as Regent's Clubs, and bringing alumni together when they are travelling. With thirty clubs active globally, alumni are able to network, socialize and get involved in such far-flung locations as Paris, São Paulo, Singapore, Dubai, New York, Stockholm and Moscow. Regent's Club London, the UK group, meets around the capital city during alternate months.

Working in conjunction with colleagues in Careers and Business Relations at the University, the alumni office has been able to offer many opportunities for professional development, including networking sessions, structured careers support and an informative lecture series throughout the year.

Volunteering forms the heart of alumni involvement at Regent's, whether it entails taking part in the mentoring programme, providing one-to-one sessions for postgraduate students in need of reflection and sector experience, or working through Regent's Clubs to support student recruitment activity. Regent's alumni participate readily in improving the student experience, and now also form a significant provider of current student internships – vital components of study in many courses.

Within the context of this programme of benefits, *Inner Circle* is a flagship publication celebrating the talent and spirit of the Regent's community. The Alumni Relations team, led by David Whitaker, is committed to achieving an open, friendly style, typical of the broad international community that it brings together. They have placed emphasis on high-quality visuals and intelligent writing, underpinned by a mission to explain the new association and the life of the University and its extended community today.

Focus on Staff

People are at the heart of any successful enterprise. Regent's views its staff, students and alumni as members of the Regent's 'family', and aspires to develop the potential of each person to their maximum ability. The University seeks to maintain a culture of mutual respect, a commitment to equity and a policy of inclusion for all. For staff, this means maintaining an active development programme for the benefit of individuals and the institution itself. The Human Resources Director, Sue Shutter, has led the development of an innovative Performance Development Review process that seeks to set clear objectives, monitor progress on their achievement and provide developmental support to maximize the probability of success. This process has been refined year by year since its introduction, and its positive impact can now be seen across the University.

Regent's wishes to be an employer of choice for the best staff in higher education. In order to assess success in moving towards this goal, an independent staff survey is commissioned every eighteen months. The most recent survey showed a massive improvement in staff satisfaction over the five years from 2007 to 2012, a clear understanding of and support for Regent's development strategy, and a genuine collegiate spirit.

To help strengthen the understanding of staff, a Staff Conference is held annually. Schools and departments share information about their activities, debates take place on key developments, and there are cross-institution team-building exercises. The conference is voluntary to attend, and all permanent and visiting members of staff are invited. In the first year of the conference, 2011, about 25 per cent of staff participated; in 2013, over 65 per cent of an enlarged staff attended.

A major portfolio of programmes is offered through the Development team. In addition to providing activities directly related to staff roles, Regent's counsels and encourages staff to maintain their own career development and lifelong learning. Language learning is offered free of charge, and Regent's sponsors staff to take further academic or professional qualifications either at the University itself or elsewhere.

College to University

The 2020 Vision

In late 2010 the Chair of the Board of Trustees and the Chief Executive reviewed progress against the strategic plan developed in 2007. They recognized that, while progress had been better than projected, the face of higher education in the United Kingdom, in Europe and globally was changing rapidly, and turbulent times lay ahead. It was decided that the Board and Directorate would be failing in their duties if they did not carry out a radical review of the options going forward in order to identify possible risks and opportunities.

At a Board Meeting on 9 February 2011, the Trustees and Directorate discussed a variety of options for the future College strategy. These ranged from simply proceeding with the then current direction, becoming smaller and more specialist or merging with a larger institution through to the growth of Regent's into a full university with delivery on more than one site. Through the first six months of 2011, in an iterative consultation with the Board, the

Directorate worked through an analysis of probable developments, implications for the College, development options and the risks of different models.

At a Regent's Board Meeting in July 2011 these options were discussed and the Directorate was then asked to develop a single new strategy that accommodated the comments and suggestions of the Board. This led to a paper called 'The 2020 Vision', which proposed some major changes to the previous strategy.

At the core of the proposal was a continuing commitment to the central elements of the College's direction. It was felt that there was no need to alter the main substance of Regent's mission, values and vision. There was also a commitment to maintain the core elements of the College's pedagogy, including an international focus, a small feel, predominantly face-to-face learning, high contact hours, a low student–staff ratio, personal attention and a strong focus on employability.

Ambitious plans for further growth sat at the heart of the new strategy, which set out

The reception desk at Reid Hall, a student residence. Long-serving member of staff and popular University character William Carbury is on the far right of the picture.

a programme for increasing student numbers from fewer than 4000 in 2011 to approximately 8000 students by 2020. The growth is to be achieved in a variety of ways: the organic growth of existing programmes, extending the portfolio and establishing new schools with complementary subjects; the acquisition of small institutions with similar missions and which possess assets and programmes complementary to the Regent's portfolio; the establishment of international campuses in key developing locations around the world, either independently or in partnership with others; and the possible development of a small federal university with small, respected, non-competitive institutions that would hold the same mission and through which costs could be reduced by sharing services.

The 2020 Vision firmly restated the College's intention to maintain its private, non-state-funded, not-for-profit status as a charity, and pledged to increase the level of the public benefit and outreach activities already provided. There was a commitment to instilling a sense of social responsibility and action in all students and staff alongside encouraging their career success. The overarching objective is to become the leading private, not-for-profit university in Europe and beyond.

The 2020 Vision also noted the belief that a successful university should have a broad portfolio to enable students to develop a wider perspective than the subject that they are studying alone. There should also be a commitment to scholarly activity and research, to inform and refresh its programmes, and to attract the best academic staff. Accordingly, the 2020 Vision projected gaining Research Degree Awarding Powers by 2020.

In the early spring of 2013 the College was granted full university title as Regent's University London (see pages 110–12); made its first acquisition, of the American InterContinental University London (see pages 112–14); and increased its student number to more than 5000.

The 2013 Fashion Show was part of the Regent's Arts Festival, and took place in a giant marquee on the lawns.

Focus on the Student Experience

During their time at the University, all students should have an exceptional experience, whether they are entering straight from school, starting their studies later in their careers or undertaking further professional development. This experience should not be limited simply to the confines of the course on which they are enrolled, but should also include the opportunity to investigate other topics, to pursue an active social life, to gain knowledge of the culture and heritage of a different location, and to make a network of friends and contacts that will last for the rest of their lives.

The ambience of the Regent's Park campus and the other buildings close by in Marylebone is one of peace and serenity, creating a first-class learning environment. Regent's maintains its commitment to providing easily accessible first-class resources to its staff and students.

The pedagogical approach is one of personal attention and support through a weekly average of twenty contact hours of different kinds, with face-to-face learning in small groups. This is supported by cutting-edge use of technology to supplement other activities and to provide easy digital access to a breadth of materials.

The London campus, in the heart of a Royal Park, is situated at the centre of one of the world's greatest cosmopolitan capital cities. Regent's can use London and its surroundings as an extended campus. The University has excellent relations with key institutions throughout the capital, including finance and commerce houses, museums and galleries, theatres, film and media organizations, the fashion and retail industries and government. These contacts are used to extend the range of options and experiences available.

Employability on graduation is recognized as a key issue for students. The Careers and Business Relations department, led by Matthias Feist, works closely with the programme directors, employers and alumni to prepare students to secure their first or next job. The successes and entrepreneurial achievements of alumni are followed with interest and used to help students' understanding of how to get ahead. The University is particularly proud of the support received from alumni who use

Hubertus Halmburger
President of the Student Union, 2009–10

My time as President of Regent's College Student Union helped to shape my studies and gave me the opportunity to develop my communication and negotiation skills. The learning curve is steep because you are facing new and unexpected challenges day by day. I recommend anyone wishing to put their leadership and negotiating skills into practice, and who cares about student life, to consider working as part of the Student Union. Not only will you be putting something back into Regent's, but also you will be taking with you developed skills that will help you to succeed in both your private and your business life.

Students gather for the annual Freshers' Fayre.

their own recent experience to help mentor graduating students.

Regent's expects its students to have an engaging social life outside their studies. The University itself provides an extensive range of events throughout the year, including the Jean Monnet Memorial Lecture (in association with the European Commission), the Europe in the World annual debate, a wide variety of international relations presentations with key speakers, and Speakers in the Park, an initiative that saw Regent's invite a number of high-profile figures to give talks to staff and students. As well as organizing social events on campus and in London's club venues, the Student Union facilitates activities as diverse as polo, photography, music and debating.

The University's aim is to provide a memorable and rewarding experience for its family members, and it is always eager to welcome them back on campus and to offer further support as their careers develop.

Crucial to the unity of the Regent's community was the creation of a student organization that properly represented the whole of the student body. For many years, the individual schools had – and to some extent still retain – their own Student Councils: elected or selected representatives who made the students' case to staff about issues and problems. Indeed, the Student Councils of the RBS and EBS undergraduate programmes were often more active than any wider grouping of student representation. Over time, however, and definitely by the mid-2000s, the College-wide Student Union came into its own as the key forum for student representation. Officers of the Student Union were members of various Senate committees and other bodies across the campus. During the time of most rapid development, the successive presidents of the Student Union have been Hubertus Halmburger (German, 2009–10), Jessica Hamilton-Hagley (British, 2010–11), Kristine Bakk (Norwegian, 2011–12), Martha Gausdal (Norwegian, 2012–13) and Gilmar Queiros (Brazilian, 2013–14). The activities of the Student Union and the integration of the student body within the representational structure of the College have been enhanced by the recent creation of the post of Dean of Students as a key member of the College's Directorate.

Martha Gausdal
President of the Student Union, 2012–13

I think I felt like everyone else when I arrived at the campus for the first time – astonished by the beautiful scenery! I thought everything was very shiny and pretty, and I was scared that my wet shoes would stain the floor. I remember my friend telling me how I would feel at home here, and I thought so too – an instinct that was proved exactly right.

The campus is small and looks a bit antique in style. It makes you feel that there is no campus around London like Regent's. I love knowing the names of so many who work at Regent's, because you see them all the time.

Gilmar Queiros
President of the Student Union, 2013–14

Contrary to most students, I went with my gut feeling and enrolled at Regent's University without visiting the campus. Regent's claimed to have all the assets necessary for my higher education, and I trusted its reputation. I can now testify that I couldn't have made a better decision. I stand amazed on a daily basis when experiencing the wonderful facilities of such a well-integrated campus.

Studying in the heart of London is certainly a privilege. Yet, another great feature of this particular campus is its amazing international community. Regent's embraces such a diverse student body, which is indeed reflected on every inch of campus.

In 2008 the charity Trees for Cities, represented by the popular commercial radio DJ Dr Fox, awarded the title 'Great Tree of London' to a magnificent plane in the University grounds.

Commitment to Public Benefit

As a charity, Regent's is committed to public benefit. At its annual strategic planning meeting in April 2013, the Board confirmed that the central characteristics of Regent's are that it is 'Independent, International and Socially Responsible' and that 'public benefit', in the broadest sense, is a major part of this responsibility.

The guidance from the Charity Commission on the meaning of public benefit is not prescriptive. The trustees of the institution must ensure that they establish a portfolio of support and services, within the framework of its objects, that will meet the reasonable expectations of the Charity Commission. Within the articles of Regent's University London, its charitable objects are:

The advancement of education for the public benefit, and the foundation, maintenance and support of an educational college or colleges for students both male and female, including residential accommodation and all necessary and proper ancillary services for such establishment.

The Trustees and staff believe strongly that education is a public benefit in itself. However, they also recognize that the University has a duty to make its skills, programmes and resources available to potential students from financially disadvantaged backgrounds, to the communities around the campus and indeed internationally where possible.

In 2012 Regent's appointed an Outreach Manager, Irene Uwejeyah, to help to develop the public benefit strategy and to ensure that all the many activities are co-ordinated and carried out effectively.

At the core of the strategy is the provision of bursaries for students from financially disadvantaged backgrounds who would not normally be able to pay the fees. These bursaries provide complete fee waivers for the length of the recipients' studies and additional funds for study abroad and learning materials. In the long term the University's strategy is to become a fees-blind institution, where prospective students will be judged initially on their potential and motivation before consideration of ability to pay fees. This will

An opportunity for quiet study in the University Library.

require the development of endowment funds, and a fundraising initiative has commenced.

In 2012 Regent's was shortlisted for the 'Widening Participation Initiative of the Year' at the Times Higher Education Awards, for its work in providing access opportunities. It was the first private institution ever to be shortlisted for the award.

The University is now developing strong relationships with local schools to help them to strengthen their academic inputs and to provide a bridge between schools and universities, and to encourage applications by more students. This is being achieved by master classes and on-campus events to help to explain the career benefits of a degree and demystify university life for potential students and their parents.

Each year Regent's enters a team in the Model United Nations in New York, at which groups from many different institutions represent a country allocated to them and must argue its case in a UN environment. The Regent's teams have always been very successful in this event; it is a valuable experience for students to

Jason Drew
BA European Business Administration, 1988

Studying at Regent's was a privilege not only because of the wonderful surroundings, but also because of the passion of the staff, including George Igler, Francis Halliwell, Paul Ream, Nick Bowen, Frank Siegmund and all the other teachers – as well as, of course, the then leader of the School, Peter Coen. At the time, the basement of what is now Tuke Hall looked ideal for a student common room. After a bit of organizing, we created the Student Council and, with a lot of help from students, a donation from EBS, a load of rollers, brushes and magnolia paint, and a dozen trips to Ikea, we were set up! We had our own fully furnished space in the School for the first time.

Many of the students from those years are still frequently in touch with one another, as indeed we are with the staff. Perhaps it was being part of a pioneering student body that led us to retain those close ties with one another and the School.

Commitment to sustainability is a keynote at Regent's. This eco-compactor generates superb compost for use on the grounds, and honey from the beehives is used by the catering staff.

understand the perspectives of other countries and cultures. The University is now organizing a Model United Nations for schools on its campus to help pre-university students to gain a more global perspective.

Regent's is also reaching out to the community to provide a focal point for local activities, and inviting local residents to participate in more activities on the site. In addition, the University hopes to help strengthen the Regent's Park educational village and ensure that the park remains a focus of continuing excellence for higher education in London.

The students at Regent's engage substantially in raising money for other charities. During the next few years it is intended that the contributions that students make to the community shall be recognized as an additional certificate that they will receive alongside their degree.

Sustainability

The University has a strong commitment to the environment that is supported by staff and students alike. In the last five years it has increased its recycling of waste considerably, resulting in more than 95 per cent recycling, a reduction to one waste-revival lorry each week, and no waste going into landfill. All organic waste is composted and is used to sustain the environment in the grounds.

Energy use has been substantially reduced by replacing old-fashioned boilers, installing natural peat roofing, replacing windows and fitting automatic presence-sensitive and long-life light systems. Water is filtered and bottled on site to reduce delivery-vehicle movements. The University has a first-rate dedicated grounds team led in 2013 by Robin Frew. The team has made the gardens more environmentally friendly by replacing low-maintenance shrubs with flowering plants and shrubs to encourage beneficial insects and bees. The University has its own hives, which produce Regent's Park Honey. The gardens also contribute produce of more than twenty types that are used

The acquisition of Taught Degree Awarding Powers in 2012 was great cause for celebration at Regent's, and attracted widespread media interest.

in the University's catering. One of the trees in the grounds is recognized as a 'Great Tree of London' – a majestic plane that is probably the oldest in the city. The University sustains the memories of staff and students who have passed away by planting memorial trees in the grounds.

Regent's efforts have been recognized externally. The University has achieved the ISO 14001 standard (Environmental management), and in 2010 was the recipient of the Platinum Award at the Mayor of London's Green500 awards. In 2012 it was shortlisted for the 'Outstanding Estates Team' award at the Times Higher Education Leadership and Management (THELMA) Awards.

Staff are encouraged to reduce emissions in London by cycling to the campus. Loans are available to purchase bicycles, and additional cycle racks have been installed. Looking forward, the University hopes to develop a new centre on its park site. It has worked hard with Professor Alan Short of Short and Associates and the University of Cambridge to design an iconic building that is in keeping with its planned location, entirely carbon neutral and respectful of the park's flora and fauna.

Gaining Degree Powers

The attainment of Taught Degree Awarding Powers (TDAP) is a testament to the maturity of an institution, the quality of its staff and its experience, and a demonstration of the quality of every aspect of its operations. In early 2007 Professor Aldwyn Cooper was charged with gaining TDAP, and this was established as an objective in Regent's first strategic plan, with a goal of making a submission in 2012 and gaining the powers in 2014.

In response to this objective, a careful study was made of the criteria that needed to be exceeded, and the Directorate started to map the College against these criteria and to identify any areas of weakness. In total there were fifty criteria, in four key groups relating to governance and academic management; academic standards and Quality Assurance; scholarship and the pedagogical effectiveness of academic staff; and the environment supporting the delivery of taught higher education programmes.

In Britain, initial application for degree-awarding powers must be made to the Privy

A procession of new graduates from the Faculty of Humanities, Arts and Social Sciences in 2012.

Council. The formal application must be accompanied by a Critical Self-Analysis (CSA) document that articulates how the institution meets the criteria, where it believes itself to be strong, where it may need further development and the plans to implement this development. As stated in the preface to the CSA, when the College submitted its application it was convinced that 'we are ready to assume responsibility for the granting of our own taught degrees'. The key to this confidence was that, as the College noted, 'we have undertaken a complete restructure of our governance, management and academic structure to ensure clarity of strategy and consistency of approach, as befits a fully integrated higher education institution'. The Privy Council passes such applications to the Department for Business, Innovation and Skills (BIS), to determine whether the institution has shown evidence that it should be considered. If the judgement is positive, the application is sent to the Quality Assurance Agency for Higher Education (QAA) to establish that there is a prima facie case and, if so, to set up a scrutiny panel to carry out a full academic

cycle review. From 2007 onwards the executive team at Regent's used each external institutional accreditation exercise as a rehearsal for preparing the submission to the Privy Council.

In April 2009 Professor Cooper met Dr Irene Ainsworth, Head of Degree Awarding Powers and University Title at the QAA, to consult on the details of the process and to gain advice on making an application. Dr Ainsworth and her colleagues provided invaluable advice then and throughout the process.

In October Cooper established a programme board to have oversight of the process of applying for TDAP. A number of external advisers were appointed on account of their experience. These included Professor David Baker, who had led the College of St Mark and St John in Plymouth to gain TDAP; Professor Julie Lydon, the Vice Chancellor of the then University of Glamorgan; Professor Peter Hodson, who had acted as chair of QAA scrutiny panels at other institutions; and Linda Cookson, who had been Head of Quality at the Central School of Speech and Drama as it had gone through the process. In early November

The graduation ceremony for the Faculty of Business and Management at Southwark Cathedral in 2011.

Regent's appointed Kate Stoneman to act as Project Manager for College Development.

During the next nine months, staff were briefed fully and consulted, and over 100 people contributed to the development of the CSA document, which went through three iterations. The substantial additional material was assembled, mapped and cross-referenced by Stoneman. In July 2010, on the recommendation of the Directorate, the Trustee Board approved the submission of the formal application to the Privy Council.

The QAA Advisory Committee on Degree Awarding Powers (ACDAP) reviewed Regent's application at its meeting in September 2010. The committee agreed that there was a prima facie case to consider the College. Dr Ainsworth then appointed a chair of the scrutiny panel, Professor Robert Harris, and a team of scrutineers. The panel commenced visits in December 2010, and in the period through to September 2011 attended the College fifty-one times for visits varying from half a day to two days in order to observe meetings with groups of staff and to review documentation. A final report was agreed in March 2012.

The ACDAP reviewed the report in late March 2012. The committee requested additional information, which was submitted quickly; the committee considered Regent's on 8 June, and on 26 June a recommendation was finally made by the QAA Board to the Minister for Universities and Science, David Willetts, that Regent's should be granted TDAP. The officers at BIS were extremely helpful, and the Chair of the Board of Trustees received notification from the Privy Council on 16 July that powers had been granted and would commence on 1 September 2012.

The process for gaining TDAP is, and should be, a testing experience. It is essential that the United Kingdom maintains its high quality standards. At that point, in 2012, Regent's was only the sixth private institution to gain this status. While the process was time-consuming and required staff to contribute above and beyond expectations, it was a valuable exercise in developing the collegiate nature of the institution. Staff across the College were forced to collaborate closely with one another. They learned a great deal about other schools and departments, which

further eroded any historic misunderstandings and set a firm foundation for future development as a university.

Gaining University Title

In the past, institutions that gained TDAP would normally have submitted an application to BIS for award of 'university college' title and then, after some years, when they had met all the criteria for full university title, would submit another application for final approval by the Privy Council. Prior to 2012, the criteria required a minimum of 4000 students, a period of experience in managing degree powers in-house and, further in the past, demonstrable research output and a breadth of provision.

In 2012, in response to lobbying by GuildHE, a body representing small, high-calibre, specialist institutions in such fields as agriculture, music, drama, art and design and some smaller regional colleges, the government approved changes to the criteria for gaining university title. Under the new regulations, an institution must have its own degree

powers. It must have a minimum of 1000 full-time equivalent (FTE) students, of whom at least 750 are registered on degree courses, representing more than 55 per cent of the entire student body at all levels. The institution must show an enhanced level of governance and financial sustainability. Finally, it must demonstrate that it has consulted widely on its proposed name and that there is no sustainable objection.

Following the introduction of these changes, approximately a dozen smaller state-funded institutions applied to the Privy Council for university title in the late summer of 2012. The majority of these institutions have now been confirmed as universities. Two private institutions also applied for title, Regent's College and the then College of Law, which had recently become a 'for profit' institution funded by external venture capital. As both institutions were private, they were required to apply through a different route, via oversight by BIS, the Higher Education Funding Council for England (HEFCE), the QAA and, in the case of Regent's, the Charity Commission. For Regent's and the College of Law, the final decision

Colleagues gather to celebrate the success of their students at the BaM Faculty graduation ceremony in 2011.

rested with the Minister for Universities and Science. The University of Law was approved in October 2012.

Although Regent's was close to meeting the old criteria for university title, its application was delayed by two issues. BIS had never before had to consider such a complex institution as Regent's, which offers both UK and American degrees, and so additional procedures needed to be established. In addition, because Regent's was in the process of making a major acquisition (the American InterContinental University London), HEFCE required additional independent reassurance that this would not threaten the long-term sustainability of the institution. Once again, the BIS officers were immensely helpful, and assistance throughout the process was also supplied by Sir Alan Langlands, Chief Executive of HEFCE; Tim Melville-Ross, Chair of the HEFCE Board; Anthony McClaran, Chief Executive of QAA; and Andy Westwood, Chief Executive of GuildHE. Regent's was informed on 19 March 2013 of the decision of BIS to grant title under the chosen name, Regent's University London (RUL).

This made Regent's the first private, non-state-funded university since the University of Buckingham was approved by Margaret Thatcher. It is only the second ever, and is far and away the largest private university provider of campus-based programmes in Britain.

Gaining full university title is of considerable benefit to any higher education institution, to its graduates, alumni and staff. Regent's will now be recognized by more national and professional bodies around the world, and will be able to participate in broader consultations and discussions than before. This recognition assists students in applying for further study elsewhere and in applying for employment throughout the world. The increased credibility and profile of the University also help in the recruitment of the best academic and professional services staff and in strengthening Regent's global network of partners.

Regent's recognizes the outstanding contributions to the sector made by the many small specialist institutions that have now gained university status in Britain. However, the University's view is that, in order to deliver

a full university experience, an institution needs
to offer a broad portfolio of programmes and a
commitment to research, and this can be managed
only through larger institutions, which are certainly
more sustainable than smaller ones.

A First Acquisition

The 2020 Vision contains a clear commitment to
the acquisition of small institutions with similar
missions and which possess assets and programmes
complementary to the Regent's portfolio. In
scanning the London higher education market,
Regent's had learned that a fellow member
of GuildHE, the American InterContinental
University London (AIUL), faced a decline in
student numbers that was leading to an untenable
financial position. After discussion with the
Regent's Chairman, the Chief Executive contacted
the AIUL campus Director, Randolph Cooper, in
October 2011, to enquire whether the owners of
the institution, AIU Atlanta and ultimately Career
Education Corporation (CEC) of Chicago, might
be interested in an approach, to mutual benefit.

Randolph Cooper arranged an initial
discussion with the Chief Financial Officer of
CEC, who confirmed that AIUL was no longer a
strategic priority for the corporation and that it
would be happy to enter discussions. The possible
acquisition was discussed further by the Regent's
Trustee Board, and negotiations commenced under
a formal confidentiality agreement.

The rationale for the acquisition was based
on a number of factors. AIUL held leases on
numerous attractive buildings within easy walking
distance of the Inner Circle campus. Owing to
falling student numbers, these buildings were
less than half-occupied and could provide much-
needed space to relieve pressure on the main site,
to permit the development of specialist media
facilities, and allow for planned expansion. In
addition, there was overall synergy on many of
the programmes that complemented the Webster
degrees offered by Regent's and were consistent
with the plans to offer dual-validated programmes.
Finally, the successful Fashion, Architectural Design
and Visual Communications areas would allow the
establishment of a new school in the HASS Faculty

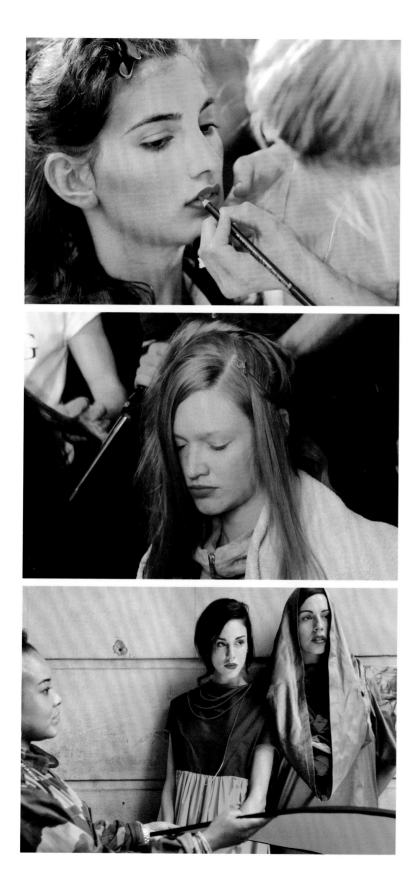

to sit alongside the London School of Film, Media and Performance and expand the portfolio.

Following initial discussions, two members of CEC staff were delegated to manage the negotiations. A programme board was established at Regent's, and the acquisition was set up as a full-scale project. As a 'for profit' company quoted on the NASDAQ exchange, CEC was concerned about confidentiality and reporting requirements. The project became known as 'Project Victoria', and knowledge of the discussions was limited to a very small group of people in both organizations.

Regent's appointed a number of external advisers to carry out comprehensive due diligence on financial, legal and property matters. The due diligence and negotiations continued throughout 2012. The intention was to bring the for-profit AIUL inside the charity as soon as possible. A teach-out agreement was prepared jointly and was submitted in November 2012 to the North Central Higher Learning Commission (NCHLC), accreditors for CEC, for its approval. A five-year business plan for what would become the Regent's group was prepared and discussed and tested by

Examples of fine fashion design from the graduation show at the American InterContinental University London in 2013. AIUL is now part of Regent's University.

the Regent's Board. Eventually, in December, a share purchase agreement was approved, with a target date for completion at the end of March. The NCHLC approved the teach-out agreement, and the acquisition took place as planned on 1 April 2013.

The programme board for what is now known as Regent's Marylebone, a wholly owned subsidiary of Regent's University London, continues to operate and has oversight of the transition for students, staff and assets. Under the terms of the teach-out agreement, those students who could qualify to graduate from the old AIUL by June 2014 were able to do so. Consultation was held individually with all the other students, and the majority transferred to Regent's. Consultations were also held with all the old AIUL staff during the summer of 2013, and the majority were transferred to Regent's terms and conditions.

Fashion, Architectural Design and Visual Communications were brought together as a school within the new structure of the University. Regent's appointed Gill Stark, one of the departmental heads within AIUL, as Head of the new Regent's School of Fashion and Design, and it is expected that this school will grow substantially in the years ahead.

Regent's University London

As preparation for gaining university title, the management commissioned an external consultancy, Lloyd Northover, to review the understanding of Regent's and the ways in which it represented itself and communicated with key stakeholders. The result of that study was the realization that the new University would need to resolve its structure, reinforce its central strengths and adopt a new visual representation to clarify its position and status. This led to the development of a new structure, a revised positioning statement (see opposite) and a new visual style. All of these were launched on 29 June 2013 at a ceremony to install the University's first Chancellor, Professor John Drew, and to celebrate the new institution with the Regent's family, friends, international partners, the higher education sector and local communities.

The Regent's Positioning Statement

We are Regent's University. We're a very special seat of learning, developing a special kind of individual, people who are succeeding in making a very real mark in the world we live in.

We're independent and we're not for profit. This means our sole focus is on ensuring that the standard of teaching, the quality of the environment and the student experience are outstanding. In the evolving higher education landscape, one day more universities might do the same.

At our London campus, the immediate environment and the city beyond provide a rich extension of the classroom. The historic Royal Park delivers a serene studying environment. The beating heart of the West End provides everything you need for your day-life and nightlife, in fact the very best of London-life is all around you. Across our growing global family of campuses we aim to create environments that are special enough to provide a community that delivers our students the best.

Teaching is in small groups with high contact hours, so you'll build a powerful relationship with your tutors. The ambience is both challenging and comfortable, intimate, safe and supportive. So you'll be able to deal with and embrace everything this transformational stage of your life places in your path. Our University schools are specialist and world-renowned, so you can be sure that, whatever you've chosen to study, the education you receive will be exceptional.

With more than 140 nationalities, our community is truly international. It provides a cultural richness without boundaries that exchanges perspectives, shares experiences and promotes dialogue. When you leave us, you'll know who you are and be able to perform confidently anywhere in the world.

But that's not all. You'll build a network and friendships that will equip you to dare just a little bit more in your life's ambitions. At Regent's University it's a world of difference, and we'll make a world of difference to your future, bringing your dreams as well as your goals just a little bit nearer.

Regent's University: your world of difference

Mayali Talwar

MA Global Management, 2010

Deciding to study here was one of the best decisions of my life. The MA in Global Management entailed a great combination of interactive, practical and theoretical learning. Not only has it helped me to gain employment in one of the best companies in India, but also it's given me the confidence to avail of other options. … I have thoroughly enjoyed my Masters programme, and would not swap it for anything else. The knowledge I gained and the relationships I formed, I take with me with immense fondness and pride.

FACULTY OF BUSINESS AND MANAGEMENT

European Business School London

Regent's Business School London

❁

FACULTY OF HUMANITIES, ARTS AND SOCIAL SCIENCES

Regent's American College London
Regent's School of Drama, Film and Media
Regent's School of Fashion and Design
Regent's School of Psychotherapy and Psychology

❁

Regent's Institute of Languages and Culture

The faculties and schools were restructured in 2013 following the award of university title and the acquisition of AIUL.

The Future for Regent's University London

The future for Regent's University London (RUL) is very positive. Its development from a small college less than thirty years ago into a growing university is an astonishing achievement, and the boundless enthusiasm and dedication within the institution suggest that it will overcome any reasonable short-term and medium-term issues.

The acquisition of the American InterContinental University in spring 2013 was a further demonstration of Regent's developed maturity as a higher education institution. As Professor Aldwyn Cooper noted early in 2013:

> This is an exciting development for the College. It will enable us to continue to develop our first-class learning experience for all by providing more space and better facilities within our central London location. We will be in a position to offer a broader range of programmes – starting with a new School of Fashion and Design. What makes this acquisition particularly special is that we are essentially turning a for-profit institution into a

not-for-profit operation as an integrated part of Regent's. While announcements like this can be unsettling for staff and students, we are delighted by the initial reactions of staff and students alike. I am confident that everybody at AIU London who chooses to join Regent's College will find their academic experience most rewarding.

The significance of the acquisition of university title and the formal change of name on 4 April 2013 to Regent's University London cannot be overestimated. The 2020 Vision is in itself a challenge, but one worth facing in the short to medium term. The strategy implies a considerable amount of growth in both number of students (an increase to approx. 8000 students) and range of activities. One of the most important challenges is in ensuring that the University retains its small feel and the individual attention and personal support to which it has always been committed.

Regent's is starting to take its place as a recognized contributor to and an important part of the increasingly diverse higher education sector in the United Kingdom, and is gaining representation on key bodies.

RUL celebrated its new status with a wonderful launch event on 29 June 2013; see pages 14–19. In addition, RUL took on the titles appropriate to becoming a university, with Professor John Drew being appointed as Chancellor and Professor Aldwyn Cooper becoming Vice Chancellor (rather than Principal); Cooper also retains the title of Chief Executive.

Regent's engaged Lloyd Northover in a new branding exercise in 2012–13, with the aim of becoming the leading internationally focused university in Europe. Within this new branding for the institution as a whole, it is accepted that some issues need to be resolved, including consideration of the fact that schools within the HASS Faculty are substantially different from one another, and that brand champions are needed for the EBS and RBS brands within the BaM Faculty.

The final word on RUL has to be a celebration of the long and successful progress of the institution from a small, pioneering college to an ambitious university with an outward-looking and progressive view of its own future. The shape of higher education over the coming years and decades may be transformed by the success of RUL as it takes the next key steps in its own development. RUL is distinguished by its creation of an educational process that combines international outlook with professional attitudes and behaviour. It is this process that marks out RUL graduates as leaders for the twenty-first century.

Timeline

1920
The wearing of gowns by students at lectures is made compulsory.

1927
9 June HRH Princess Mary lays the foundation stone for the Tuke Building.

1908
Bedford College secures the Crown lease of South Villa.

1929
December Margaret Tuke retires as Principal.

1827
Decimus Burton designs and builds South Villa on the University's site.

1909
South Villa is put to use for resident students.

1810	1820	1830	1900	1910	1920	1930

1811
Farming leases in Marylebone Park expire.

1835
Members of the public are allowed into the park.

1911
The building of Bedford College begins.

1930
March The Observatory opens.

Summer South Villa is demolished.

1818
John Nash develops Regent's Park.

1913
2 July Lord Eversley writes to *The Times*, complaining about the 'eyesore' in the park.

4 July HM Queen Mary officially opens Bedford College.

1931
24 June HM Queen Mary officially opens the Tuke Building.

1914
1 August The First World War breaks out.

1939
The Second World War breaks out, and the College evacuates to Cambridge.

1915–16
The staff and students support the war effort by preparing drugs, forming an Allotment Society and hosting parties for the wives and mothers of serving men.

1919
The presentation of degrees resumes after discontinuation during the war, and degrees are awarded to graduates from 1916, 1917 and 1918.

1951
January Builders complete the Herringham Building.

1952
28 October The College holds 'Reconstruction Celebrations'.

1955
HM Queen Elizabeth The Queen Mother visits the College.

1984
May HM Queen Elizabeth The Queen Mother pays a farewell visit to the College.

Rockford College takes over the lease of the site from the Crown Estate.

1985
2 September The first students arrive at Regent's College.

The telescope is removed from the Observatory.

The European Business School takes up residence on the campus.

2006
6 March Regent's Business School becomes part of Regent's College.

June The College becomes a single corporate body and establishes the College Senate.

2007
January Professor Aldwyn Cooper becomes Chief Executive of the College.

1940	1950	1960	1980	1990	2000	2010

1941
10 May Air raids inflict irreparable damage on one-third of the College buildings.

1944
The College returns to Regent's Park.

1946
The College leases The Holme for additional space.

1947
Re-building work begins, and the buildings are renamed.

1962–64
The Wernher Reading Room is demolished and replaced by the three-storey Jebb Building.

1965
October Bedford College admits male undergraduates for the first time.

1990
Regent's College establishes the School of Psychotherapy and Counselling.

1994
The College agrees a partnership with Webster University and establishes the Webster Graduate School and the British American College London.

1997
Regent's Business School is established.

2011
The first Staff Conference is held.

2012
The Privy Council awards Taught Degree Awarding Powers to Regent's College.

2013
19 March The Department for Business, Innovation and Skills approves Regent's for university title.

1 April Regent's College acquires the American InterContinental University London.

4 April Regent's College officially changes its name to Regent's University London.

20 May Regent's begins validating all its own taught programmes.

29 June Regent's University London installs its first Chancellor and unveils its new visual identity during a celebration in the grounds.

International Partners

ARGENTINA

Universidad Argentina de la Empresa *P*

Universidad de San Andrés *P*

Universidad del CEMA *P*

Universidad Torcuato Di Tella *P*

AUSTRALIA

Deakin University *P*

Queensland University of Technology *P*

RMIT University *P*

University of Technology Sydney *P*

AUSTRIA

Johannes Kepler Universität *P*

University of Salzburg Business School *P*

BAHRAIN

Capital Knowledge *P*

BELGIUM

Solvay Brussels School of Economics and Management *P*

BRAZIL

Fundação Getulio Vargas *P*

UniSEB Centro Universitário *P*

CANADA

Concordia University *P*

CREPUQ *P*

Université du Québec à Montréal *P*

Université Laval *P*

CHILE

Pontificia Universidad Católica de Chile *P*

Universidad Adolfo Ibáñez *P*

CHINA

Beijing Language and Culture University *P*

Nanjing University *P*

Qingdao University *P*

Tsinghua University *P*

Zhejiang Gongshang University *P*

CZECH REPUBLIC

Divadelní Fakulta Akademie Múzických Umení (DAMU) *P*

DENMARK

Copenhagen Business School *P*

FRANCE

EDHEC Business School Lille *P*

EDHEC Business School Nice *P*

ESC Rennes School of Business *P*

ESCE Paris *P*

ESG – Ecole Supérieure de Gestion *P*

European Business School Paris *P*

IAE Graduate School of Management *P*

ISC Paris School of Management *P*

Université Nice Sophia Antipolis *P*

Université Paris-Dauphine *P*

GERMANY

EBC Hochschule *P*

Fachhochschule Worms *P*

Hochschule Neuss für Internationale Wirtschaft *P*

Hochschule Reutlingen *P*

ISM International School of Management *P*

Katholische Universität Eichstätt-Ingolstadt *P*

Munich Business School *P*

Universität Witten-Herdecke *P*

WHU Otto Beisheim School of Management *P*

ITALY

Università Ca' Foscari di Venezia *P*

Università Cattolica del Sacro Cuore *P*

Università degli Studi di Firenze *P*

Università degli Studi Roma Tre *P*

Università di Bologna *P*

Università di Pavia *P*

Sapienza Università di Roma *P*

JAPAN

Aoyama Gakuin University *P*

Hokusei Gakuen University *P*

Nanzan University *P*

Otemon Gakuin University *P*

Seinan Gakuin University *P*

LEBANON

Saint Joseph University *P*

MEXICO

Tecnológico de Monterrey *P*

MOROCCO

HEM Business School *P*

PERU

Universidad del Pacífico *P*

PORTUGAL

ISCTE Business School *P*

Universidade Católica Portuguesa *P*

RUSSIA

EBS Kaliningrad *P*

Lomonosov Moscow State University *P*

Plekhanov Russian University of Economics *P*

Russian Foreign Trade Academy *P*

St Petersburg State University *P*

SOUTH AFRICA

University of Stellenbosch Business School *P*

SOUTH KOREA

Chungnam National University *P*

Korea University *P*

SPAIN

CUNEF – Colegio Universitario de Estudios Financieros *P*

EBS Madrid – Centro Universitario Villanueva *P*

Escuela de Negocios Novacaixagalicia *P*

Universidad Antonio de Nebrija *P*

Universidad Autónoma de Madrid *P*

Universidad Católica de Valencia *P*

Universidad CEU San Pablo *P*

Universidad Complutense de Madrid *P*

Universidad de Cádiz *P*

Universidad de Castilla-La Mancha *P*

Universidad de Deusto *P*

Universidad Francisco de Vitoria *P*

Universidad Internacional de la Rioja Business School *P*

Universitat Autònoma de Barcelona *P*

Universitat de Barcelona *P*

Universitat de València *P*

Universitat Pompeu Fabra *P*

SWITZERLAND

Haute Ecole Spécialisée de Suisse Occidentale *P*

ZHAW School of Management and Law *P*

TURKEY

Istanbul Aydin University *P*

UNITED STATES

Alliant International University, San Diego, California *P*

Alma College, Alma, Michigan *A*

Anna Maria College, Paxton, Massachusetts *A*

Auburn University, Auburn, Alabama *A*

Baylor University, Waco, Texas *A*

Belmont University, Nashville, Tennessee *A*

Bethany College, Bethany, West Virginia *A*

Chestnut Hill College, Philadelphia, Pennsylvania *A*

The College of Saint Rose, Albany, New York *A*

The College of St Scholastica, Duluth, Minnesota *A*

Concordia University, Mequon, Wisconsin *A*

Daemen College, Amherst, New York *A*

DePaul University, Chicago, Illinois *P*

Drury University, Springfield, Missouri *A*

Fairfield University, Fairfield, Connecticut *A*

Florida Southern College, Lakeland, Florida *A*

Fontbonne University, St Louis, Missouri *A*

Forsyth Technical Community College, Winston-Salem, North Carolina *A*

Hartwick College, Oneonta, New York *A*

Hawaii Pacific University, Honolulu, Hawaii *P*

Hillsdale College, Hillsdale, Michigan *A*

John Carroll University, University Heights, Ohio *A*

Long Island University, Brookville, New York *A*

Lycoming College, Williamsport, Pennsylvania *A*

Madonna University, Livonia, Michigan *A*

Mars Hill College, Mars Hill, North Carolina *A*

Marymount College, Rancho Palos Verdes, California *A*

Monmouth University, West Long Branch, New Jersey *P/A*

Morningside College, Sioux City, Iowa *A*

Mount Ida College, Newton, Massachusetts *A*

New England College, Henniker, New Hampshire *A*

Nichols College, Dudley, Massachusetts *A*

Northern Illinois University, DeKalb, Illinois *A*

Pace University, New York *P*

Parsons The New School for Design, New York City *P*

Point Park University, Pittsburgh, Pennsylvania *A*

Queens University of Charlotte, Charlotte, North Carolina *A*

Quincy University, Quincy, Illinois *A*

Ramapo College of New Jersey, Mahwah, New Jersey *A*

Regis College, Weston, Massachusetts *A*

Roanoke College, Salem, Virginia *A*

Robert Morris University, Chicago, Illinois *A*

Rockford University, Rockford, Illinois *A*

Rocky Mountain College, Billings, Montana *A*

Saint Mary-of-the-Woods College, Saint Mary of the Woods, Indiana *A*

San Francisco State University, San Francisco, California *P*

Shorter University, Rome, Georgia *A*

Southern Methodist University, Dallas, Texas *A*

Southern Utah University, Cedar City, Utah *A*

Stephens College, Columbia, Missouri *A*

Suffolk University, Boston, Massachusetts *P/A*

Susquehanna University, Selinsgrove, Pennsylvania *A*

Tarleton State University, Stephenville, Texas *A*

Tiffin University, Tiffin, Ohio *A*

Transylvania University, Lexington, Kentucky *A*

Tulane University, New Orleans, Louisiana *A*

University of Hartford, West Hartford, Connecticut *A*

University of Memphis, Memphis, Tennessee *A*

University of New Hampshire, Durham, New Hampshire *A*

University of North Florida, Jacksonville, Florida *P*

University of St Francis, Joliet, Illinois *A*

Webster University, St Louis, Missouri *A*

Western New England University, Springfield, Massachusetts *A*

Westminster College, New Wilmington, Pennsylvania *A*

William Woods University, Fulton, Missouri *A*

URUGUAY

Universidad Católica del Uruguay *P*

In Memoriam

Picture Credits

Index

Contributors

Judith Ackroyd
Aldwyn Cooper
Ian Mehrtens
John Nuttall
Steve Phillips
David Whitaker

Contributing Editor
Rosalind Cooper

Researcher
Sam Cannicott

Picture Researcher
Jason Pittock

Administrative Assistant
Amna Maroof

First published 2013 by Merrell Publishers, London and New York

Merrell Publishers Limited
70 Cowcross Street
London EC1M 6EJ

merrellpublishers.com

British Library Cataloguing in Publication Data. A catalogue record for this book is available from the British Library.

ISBN 978-1-8589-4621-4

Produced by Merrell Publishers Limited
Designed by Nicola Bailey
Project-managed by Claire Chandler
Indexed by Hilary Bird

Printed and bound in Italy

Front jacket:
The main entrance to Regent's University London, August 2013.

Back jacket and pages 2–3:
An aerial view of Regent's University London shows its enviable location in the heart of Regent's Park, surrounded by trees and natural beauty.

Pages 6–7:
A late summer view of the Tuke Building, just before the Virginia creeper turns to glorious shades of red and purple.

Page 8:
The Tate Library in spring. This elegant building was constructed in 1913 and sponsored by Lady Tate, heiress to the famed sugar fortune.

Page 128:
Bluebells appear in the late spring, adding new colour to the gardens.

Endpapers:
Part of the University's new visual identity unveiled in 2013.

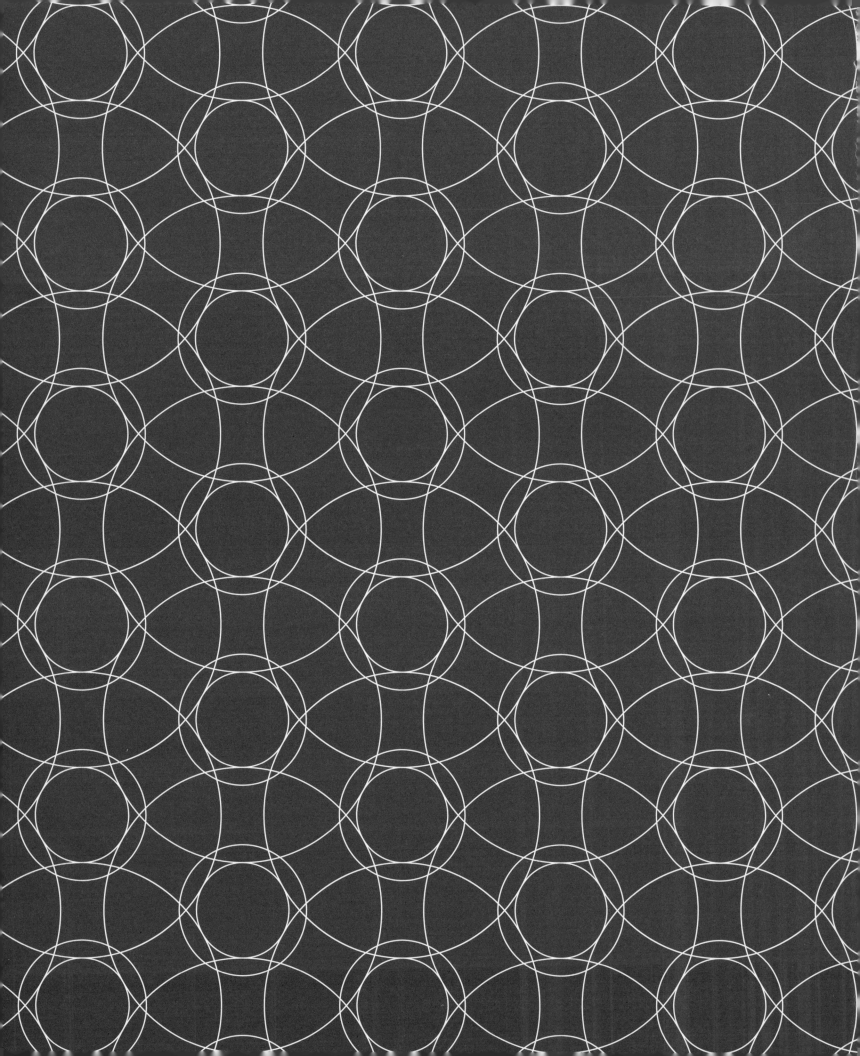